LET THE SPIRIT IN

LET THE SPIRIT IN
Practicing Christian Devotional Meditation

William E. Hulme

Abingdon   Nashville

LET THE SPIRIT IN

Copyright © 1979 by Abingdon

Library of Congress Cataloging in Publication Data

HULME, WILLIAM EDWARD. 1920–
    Let the spirit in.
    1. Meditation. I. Title.
BV4813.H6   248'.3   78-26739

ISBN 0-687-21379-7

Scripture quotations unless otherwise noted are from the Revised Standard
Version of the Bible, copyrighted 1946, 1952, © 1971, 1973 by the Division of
Christian Education of the National Council of the Churches of Christ in the
U.S.A.

MANUFACTURED BY THE PARTHENON PRESS AT
NASHVILLE, TENNESSEE, UNITED STATES OF AMERICA

Lucy, Dale, Polly,
Marcia, and Lance

CONTENTS

PREFACE

Say your prayers. Children used to hear this parental admonition on retiring to bed far more than they do today. It was an odd directive—Say your prayers—but perhaps this familiar admonition indicates more than we realized about our conception of prayer as something one "does," rather than as an experience of communion. Nor is it insignificant that the directive was given at bedtime. Night, darkness, and sleep are all symbols for death. The day is over, and the time has come to surrender our consciousness to the limbo of sleep. A popular children's prayer of the day reflected this symbolism: "Now I lay me down to sleep, I pray the Lord my soul to keep. If I should die before I wake, I pray the Lord my soul to take."

The ominous content of this prayer was mildly frightening to me as a child—not exactly a state of mind conducive to rest and sleep. By the time I became a parent myself the prayer had developed another version: "Now I lay me down to sleep, I pray the Lord my soul to keep. When in the morning light I wake, help me the path of love to take." Perhaps this new version arose because modern medicine had succeeded in postponing death to a later time of life.

Daily Devotions

From such early bedtime habits it was hoped that children would gradually develop the discipline of daily prayer—often referred to as daily devotions. "To devote" literally means to vow completely, and "devotion" in the plural is associated with personal or private prayer as differentiated from the corporate prayers said in churches.

Daily devotions usually consisted of reading the Bible and/or other devotional literature and reading or saying a prayer or prayers. The Bible was the basis for devotions since God speaks to us through his Word, and our response is through prayer. People have obviously felt the need for something more than their own ingenuity in the use of the Bible and prayer since denominational publishing houses offer an abundance of devotional materials.

Daily devotions were an important part of my own spiritual development. I grew up in a Christian home where bedtime prayers and family devotions were a regular part of family life. Following my confirmation, and perhaps due to confirmation instruction, I experienced an acceleration of religious interest during adolescence and surpassed the family devotional patterns. By the time I had finished high school I had read the Bible several times and was a missionary among my friends advocating daily devotions. The practice survived my adolescence and became a scheduled activity in my daily routine.

Despite my debt to this practice, I believe from my own observation and experience that daily devotions in their usual format have some built-in limitations. As something one does they are one activity among others in a busy day. In their denominationally prescribed models, the practice has been reduced in time and scope so as not to threaten the pace of a busy person. Titles such as "Five Minutes a Day" are indicative of this trend. In addition, daily devotions are largely "head trips," with a predominately educational emphasis. Reading the Bible is thought of as Bible study. Daily devotions

Let the Spirit In

are a western-oriented spirituality in which even quiet times are thinking times.

My criticism of daily devotions is not that they incorporate the rational dimension of our being, but rather that they largely confine us to it. We need Bible study and coherent prayers. We also need to involve other capacities of our person. Besides our analytical and rational abilities, we also have capacities for the intuitive, the artistic, and the sensuously imaginative. The complementary nature of these differing capacities form a balance in human life.

In recent years the clergy's appeal to people to maintain personal and family devotions has often seemed to fall on deaf ears—like the proverbial beating of a dead horse. Clergy themselves may at times admit to inadequacy in their devotional life. When a guilt-trip is laid on someone for this omission, the usual response is, "I know I should—but . . ." There is a lack of both time and determination. Who then could have predicted in the busy fifties or the activist sixties that a meditation boom would occur in the seventies? And ironically, meditation demands even more time than daily devotions, but some of those who could not spare the five-minutes-a-day are now positively committed to twenty minutes or more a day in meditation.

In the midst of ambivalent apathy toward daily devotions there are those for whom this practice continues to mean a great deal. In no way do I wish to detract from the value that daily devotions have for these persons; nor am I suggesting that those who are receiving sufficiently from their devotional life should abandon their practices for something else. In spite of structural predispositions, daily devotions need not be solely or even primarily cerebral in nature, as many know who are involved in the practice with their total persons. Daily devotions meant much to me even as they mean much to many now. My concern is with those religiously motivated persons who are lacking a disciplined devotional practice or who are feeling the need for something other or more than they are now practicing.

In the following chapters I want to share with you the approach to meditation and devotion that I have developed over the years and find helpful. For those who may be interested, I have described briefly in a postscript to this book the main influences in my personal and professional development that have contributed to this approach.

Chapter One
MEDITATION AND HOLISTIC HEALTH

Our age has been characterized as an age of anxiety, stress, and tension, and as a consequence of these, an age of chemical dependency. In addition to alcoholism—our fourth most prevalent disease and major addiction whose consequences are well known—there is also dependency on illegal drugs, the consequences of which continue to be exposed. Drug dependency is also a growing trend in prescription drugs such as Valium, for which 62,000,000 prescriptions were written in 1977. Withdrawal symptoms in those dependent upon Valium may reach the intensity of epilepticlike convulsions. Some users combine Valium and alcohol with potentially disastrous results. Add to these dependencies the 7,000,000,000 aspirin tablets taken in 1977—which also are not completely without negative effects —and we come face to face with a huge problem of pain. The limited use of aspirin to prevent strokes in men, currently under investigation, adds a different and intriguing dimension to the use of this drug. Ironically a side effect of aspirin—the slowing of blood coagulation—is the possible asset in the prevention of strokes.

A nonchemical addiction that is reaching epidemic proportions is television dependence. In a recent study in which specific families were paid not to use the television, the family members went through withdrawal symptoms similar to those of chemical dependency. TV, like drugs, is a "distractor" from the stress of a problematic existence.

1. *Interrelationship of Body, Mind, and Spirit*

Our anxieties often show up as psychosomatic factors in our illnesses. The fact that psychic tension can contribute to disease in the body points to the interrelationship of body, mind, and spirit. Mind and spirit are sometimes used synonymously, but I prefer to distinguish them. By mind, I mean the self as a reasoning and feeling being. By spirit, I mean the self as a worshiping being, concerned with questions of meaning and purpose and capable of religious experience.

The interrelationship of body, mind, and spirit is a specifically biblical position. During the first century, this position was in conflict with the perspectives of the surrounding world in which the dominant philosophical emphases separated mind and/or spirit from body. According to these philosophies the body was considered a limitation, even a prison, from which the mind and spirit could to some degree be emancipated through the functions of reason and contemplation. At death, the mind (or soul) would be freed from its bondage to its physically low estate. The Christian position varied sharply from such a division and interrelated body, mind, and spirit even beyond death with its teaching of the resurrection of the body.

The healing ministry of Jesus often dramatized this interrelationship. Once when he was preaching from a porch to a large crowd, the friends of a paralyzed man tried to bring their friend to Jesus for healing. They resolved their frustration over how to get to him by climbing to the thatched roof of the porch and removing the thatches; they then lowered the paralyzed man in his cot in front of Jesus as he preached.

Such determination could scarcely go unnoticed. But to the amazement of the crowd, Jesus said to the man, "Take heart, my son, your sins are forgiven." A man's friends make a bold initiative to secure healing for a paralyzed body, and Jesus responds by assuring the man that his sins are forgiven! Did he perceive a connection between a spirit immobilized by guilt and a paralyzed body? When Jesus' critics in the crowd were offended by his assertion of the authority to forgive sins, he asked them, "For which is easier, to say, 'Your sins are forgiven,' or . . . 'Rise and walk'? But that you may know that the Son of man has authority on earth to forgive sins—he then said to the paralytic—'Rise, take up your bed and go home' " (Matt. 9:5-6). While one cannot be dogmatic about interpretation, it is certainly possible that the healing of this man's body was directly connected with the healing of his spirit.

In several other accounts of his healing ministry Jesus assured those whom he healed, "Your faith has made you whole." By so saying Jesus ascribed to a spiritual attitude, faith, a healing influence for the body. Conversely, when his teaching was resisted by the people of his home area, his healing ministry was also hindered. "And he did not do many mighty works there, because of their unbelief" (Matt. 13:58). The fact that they knew him and his family as he grew up among them was an obstacle in their minds to receiving him as anything more than a fallible and limited human being like themselves. Even as faith was the means for receiving Jesus' healing ministry, so also faith's opposite, unbelief—actually, resistance to believing—was an obstacle to such reception.

Tensions in our spirit project themselves into our bodies. Many of our diseases are aggravated if not initiated by these tensions. Some of the increase in the amount of back pains people are suffering is due to the fact that spiritual or mental

Meditation and Holistic Health ◁ 15

tensions actually become muscle tensions. The therapy of bioenergetics focuses on relaxing these muscle tensions through exercises specifically designed to reach and "relax" the spirit. Rolfing and other massage therapies pursue a similar goal. The idea is that we have buried some of our traumatic memories in our knotted muscles. Relaxing these knots under the pressure of deep massage may release the memory back into consciousness. On one occasion as I was receiving a deep massage I was experiencing a great deal of pain from the masseur's thumbs. Noticing my grimaces he asked hopefully, "What are your thoughts?" All I could come up with was a memory of the pain from the dentist's drill as a child. I know I disappointed him.

Stress in the body may also adversely affect the spirit. Most of us have noticed either by experience or observation the effect of physical pain on disposition. One of my colleagues had been in chronic pain for some time. One day I noticed a change in his spirits and said, "You must be feeling better." "I am," he said, "but I didn't know it was that obvious. It is amazing what pain can do to one." Chronic pain can so absorb our attention that it turns us in on ourselves, diminishing our interest in the world about us and reducing our sensitivity to the needs of others.

Pain not only hurts physically; it can become a source of anxiety also. If pain persists, we may become depressed over it as well—will it ever go away? Depression and anxiety, though a natural result of pain, may fix or even expand the physical pain. When in pain we also tend to feel less patient and are more easily irritated. Since our crotchetiness may drive people away from us, these negativities jeopardize the support we need from others. A spiraling of stress may result from these side effects as the tensions of the spirit feed into the body, and the tensions of the body feed into the spirit.

2. Meditation and Health

It was a boost to the meditation movement when the benefits of meditation to health—physically, mentally, spiritually—became publicized. The work of Robert Keith Wallace could be considered a milestone in this regard. As a doctoral candidate in physiology, Wallace experimented with the effects of Transcendental Meditation (TM) on bodily functions. He discovered that persons in meditation have a 20 percent lower oxygen and carbon dioxide interchange than normally, indicating a lower metabolism rate. The resistance of their skin to an electric current is four times the normal, indicating an increased state of relaxation. Their heart rate is three beats less per minute, another indication of the slower pace. When Wallace tested brain waves with the electroencephalogram, he recorded alpha rays rather than beta rays. Beta rays are normally emitted when a person is involved in rational processes. Alpha rays are emitted when one slows down or even halts one's thought processes by tuning out environmental distractions and focusing mentally on nothing, or on mental images that may emerge during this state.

Wallace's published results caught the eye of Herbert Clark Benson, a cardiologist on the Harvard Medical School faculty who was working in the area of hypertension, which affects one-third of all adults in the United States. Impressed by the fact that meditation as a mental state could markedly alter physiological functions, Benson envisioned its possibilities as a counteractive to hypertension. People need help with their tensions in an age of anxiety when pressures are coming upon them from the outside and the inside. Benson's tests showed that meditation was as effective as most drugs in reducing hypertension, and without potentially dangerous side effects. In dealing with the ordinary tensions of everyday life, meditation is an improvement over tobacco, alcohol, coffee, aspirin, and Alka-seltzer. It is also an improvement over becoming a workaholic as people in the professional and business world are prone to do as a way of coping with tension. Benson subsequently ceased using Transcendental Meditation and devised his own form of meditation in which he uses the word "one" in place of a TM mantra.[1]

The publication of these studies coincided with a growing interest in holistic health. Holistic health is a term used to describe the interaction of spirit, mind, and body as it pertains to health or illness. Our attitudes, emotions, values, and priorities are all significant to the functioning of our body chemistry. Our life-style, mode of being-in-the-world, "Weltanschauung," are related to the health of our total person. By the same token, good nutrition, disciplined physical exercise, and bodily relaxation are significant to our mental and spiritual health. In holistic health there is less reliance on "invasion" therapies such as drugs and more reliance on natural therapies such as meditation.

Since the studies of Wallace and Benson were published, other studies have been undertaken which either corroborate or question their findings. A study conducted at the University of Washington on TM indicated that meditators may sleep during part of their meditation period and that the physiological findings are the same for the sleep period as for the meditative period. Similarly a study conducted at the University of Minnesota on Benson's meditative format indicated that meditators demonstrate no lasting reduction in their blood pressure, although reduction was noted during the actual meditative period. With my limited knowledge, the weight of evidence seems to be in the direction of Wallace and Benson; still it is best to be cautious in our claims for scientific evidence while research continues.

Psychiatrist William Glasser calls meditation a positive addiction. He believes that meditation has established its value in counteracting and preventing illness with psychomatic dimensions, which includes practically all illnesses. It is an addiction because as with negative addictions such as alcoholism, the user becomes habituated to meditation and feels he needs it regularly to function well. It is positive because it not only gives pleasure as addictions usually do, but also provides strength and integration, effects which are the exact opposite of negative addictions. Significantly, the other major positive addiction in Glasser's findings is running, a physical activity conducive not only to physical health, but also to mental and spiritual health as well.

3. Secularization of Meditation

One of the most obvious changes regarding meditation has been the secularization of both the word and the practice. It took me a while to realize that what a psychiatrist friend called meditation had little if anything to do with religion. For him it is a form of therapy that he uses regularly in his practice regardless of a person's religious beliefs or lack of them.

TM was originally associated with the Hindu religion in India. According to Adam Smith, when the Maharishi decided to bring it to the United States, he initially planned to associate it with our predominating religion, Christianity.[2] However, upon investigating the possibility, he concluded that science rather than religion was the vital influence in the United States. Therefore, he decided to join TM with science, calling it "The Science of Creative Living." Although he continued to include introductory Hindu rituals, TM for all practical purposes became a secular pursuit. One of the indicators of its success on the American scene was the founding of Maharishi University at Fairfield, Iowa, with Robert Keith Wallace as its first president.

I have received the introductory presentation to TM, but

decided that so far as secular meditation was concerned I preferred the unambiguously secular format of Silva Mind Control. The Silva Mind Control course teaches meditation without calling it that. Stressing a scientific base, the Silva Program is presented as a "science of the mind." The meditation exercises repeat a verbal ritual comparable to a religious liturgy as a way of "taking" one to the "inner depths of one's mind." There is an emphasis on deep breathing and on a positive attitude. The phrase "better and better" is a familiar part of the liturgy. The ritual is often referred to as "conditioning." This secular liturgy has a similar purpose to religious liturgy as a reenforcement of a point of view or a frame of mind. In line with holistic health this "science of the mind" is also used for physical healing. Participants are given mental directions for influencing the functioning of their own bodies as well as the bodies of others. Consequently an elementary knowledge of anatomy is taught in the course. The purpose of such knowledge is to provide the mind with an accurate image of body organs and functions so that one can direct them to function healthily when they are diseased or otherwise malfunctioning. In the meditative state one pictures the specifically diseased organ and then cancels that picture and substitutes an image of a healthily functioning organ and in effect directs the body to heal itself.

The Simonton Clinic in Fort Worth, Texas, utilizes a meditative format with cancer patients who are taking chemotherapy to assist the effect of that therapy. Entering into a meditative state, the patient pictures the invading chemicals attacking weak cancer cells and destroying them while healthy normal cells remain unharmed. In a similar manner meditators can imagine their disease-fighting cells attacking their own cancer cells—or other diseased cells—and picture them as winning the battle. In this way one supports the resources with which the body is endowed for resisting disease by directing these resources in the meditative state to do their job. It is a new application in the western world of the old story of mind over matter.

Mind over matter may actually be "mind producing matter." Research on the use of placebos—usually sugar or saline solutions that patients believe are potent drugs—indicates that the faith of the receiver may make the placebo "work" because a person's faith can stimulate the body to produce its own painkilling substance called endorphin, a chemical similar to morphine. It is not inconceivable that meditation could produce similar effects. By meditating upon the release from pain, one might trigger his or her body to produce its own endorphin.

Psychiatrist Glasser became interested in meditation primarily because of the positive effects he observed in the lives of meditators. Being the founder of Reality Therapy, he was disinclined toward anything mystical or religious. Once meditation had become secularized, Glasser was free as a scientific therapist to investigate it. But unhappily for him some of his meditative subjects interpreted their experiences religiously. To Glasser, religion is an unnecessary if not distorting encumbrance to meditation. Commenting on an article concerning meditation that was supportive of his position, written by two Roman Catholic priests who are social scientists, Andrew M. Greeley and William C. McCready, Glasser remarks: "Finally they [Greeley and McCready] say they have no explanation why the experiences are always joyous except a religious one that unusual forces are felt by the person as gracious and benign. This may be so, but I think a better explanation is that the process of one's brain expanding in new directions, plus gaining access to pathways that were previously denied is like getting out of jail and finding treasure."[3]

Contrary to Glasser, I believe that religion is not irrelevant to meditation. Rather, I believe that it enriches the whole experience. One is not pressed, then, as is Glasser, to explain the nonrational aspects of the experience in an unestablished if not untenable description of brain cell activity.[4] I also believe that meditation's relationship to health is enhanced by a religious understanding of humanity. There is a need to commune with more than oneself as one focuses on one's inner being. One of my teachers in secular meditation who meditated as he jogged related an incident from his own experience. He stubbed his toe as he jogged on a California beach, but continuing in the meditative state, imagined or directed healing power from his abdomen to his toe. According to his story, what might have been a painful injury failed to materialize. Significantly, he made this comment: "Then I looked up and said, 'Thank you, Universe!' and resumed my jogging."

The creature is not the Creator even though he has coveted to be such since the Garden of Eden. The awareness of our creatureliness comes not only in moments of inadequacy and helplessness as is often assumed. Even those who rationally do not recognize any distinction between creature and creator may intuitively break through with this recognition in moments of gratitude. How does one relieve one's need to thank someone? "Thank you, Universe!"

4. Influence of Eastern Religions

When we find a religious dimension to the contemporary meditation movement, it is more likely to be Eastern in character than Christian. Humanistic psychology which is the theoretical base for the Human Potential Movement has an affinity for the oneness emphasized in Eastern religions, specifically the oneness of the human and the divine. In this respect, Christian perspectives seem sharp and divisive to

Let the Spirit In

many people, not only in the division between God and man, but also between good and evil, and truth and falsehood. Then too, Christian concepts are old stuff on the American scene, while Eastern thought in its contemporary form is new—even avant-garde. Those breaking new ground are often inclined to pass over the values of their own heritage in favor of something new, for the new may also seem liberating—a liberation from "bondage" to the old.

The Christian faith itself actually has a long and rich tradition in meditation, although this tradition has not been universally practiced. Christians can of course receive much from the secularists, the humanists, and the Eastern religions. The Christian concept of the sovereignty of God permits us to receive from Him through these other means. We not only can, but have received. On the other hand, the Christian faith has its own unique contribution to make to the meditation movement. This uniqueness centers in the relational nature of Christian meditation—what Paul Tournier calls the inner dialogue.

Chapter Two
FOCUS ON THE PHYSICAL

In this chapter I hope to initiate you into the meditative process. We shall pause twice in the reading of this chapter for you to take two preparatory exercises. So you may wish to read this chapter when you have an opportunity to include additional time for the exercises.

1. *Focus on the Body*

The beginning exercises are mental focusings on your body. I have previously defined what I mean by mind and spirit, and although the meaning of body might seem obvious, it is now appropriate to clarify the significance of the body to the mind and spirit. Our body expresses our relationship to nature. As creatures we were created in the context of the total creation. We share common ground with the animals of the earth. In the Creation Story in the second chapter of Genesis, the newly created earth is described as ready for life; so God caused a "mist" to go up from the earth to water "the whole face of the ground—then the Lord God formed man of dust from the ground" (Gen. 2:6-7). The old Christian burial liturgies emphasized this identity of man with the earth. As the officiating clergy cast a handful of soil upon the casket that was being lowered into the grave, they spoke the following words, "From dust thou art and to dust thou shalt return." Since we share our life in the body with the rest of creation, our

24 ▷

animality is fundamental to any realistic understanding of human identity.

Yet Christian pieties have often rejected this aspect of our identity because of an assumed antipathy between the spirit and the body. Since the spirit is the self in its outreach to God, the body, because of its identity with nature, must be opposed to the spirit—and therefore to God. This idea of a conflict between man as spirit and man as body did not come from Christianity's Judaic roots, but from the influence of the surrounding Greek and Persian cultures in the early centuries of the Christian era. These ideas crept into Christian piety—behavior characterized by devotion to God—in spite of the fact that the church, in its early creedal decisions, affirmed the unity of God with his creation as witnessed by the Incarnation—in-the-fleshness—of his son. Even when our theology is clear in our heads, our piety can evidently pursue a contrary direction.

There is frequently a time-lag between our "seeing" something on a rational level and our "seeing" it on an emotional level. Feelings follow habit patterns and do not automatically change with each changing intellectual insight. It not only takes time for our feelings to "catch up" to our intellectual insights, but also conscious effort. In some cases, this so-called time-lag can become instead a continuing gap between our rationality, identified with our head, and our feelings, identified with our heart or gut. Nevertheless, our pieties will be shaped by our feelings as much or even more than by our intellects.

In meditation we can reaffirm our identity with nature by focusing on our bodies. There are two major areas for this bodily focus, and we will concentrate on these in this chapter. The first is our lungs, the seat of our breathing, and the second is our abdomen, the seat of our digesting. The emphasis on breathing in meditation is associated with Yoga, the

Focus on the Physical

Hindu-oriented exercises to achieve physical and spiritual well-being. The focus on the abdomen is associated with Buddhist meditation. This bodily emphasis in Eastern meditation is in harmony with the stress on listening to our bodies in holistic health. Humanistic psychology's interest in Eastern religions is also in line with the emphasis on the interrelationship of body, mind, and spirit. One of the manifestations of this emphasis is humanistic psychology's growing interest in the phenomenon of healing. For several years conferences on healing to investigate the psychological factors of illness and health have been held by humanistic psychologists.

2. Christian Influence

The focus in meditation on the lungs and the abdomen provides an example of how a Christian influence in meditation can be and is enriching to the movement, even as Christians have been assisted by other traditions in their own meditation. The focus on breathing, though Eastern, is also Christian. A Christian breathing exercise, for example, is described in the literature of the Hesychasts, a contemplative movement in the Greek Orthodox Church dating from the fifth century.

> You know, brother, how do we breathe: we breathe the air in and out. On this is based the life of the body, and on this depends its warmth. So, sitting down in your cell, collect your mind, lead it into the path of the breath, along which the air enters in, constrain it to enter the heart together with the inhaled air, and keep it there. Keep it there, but do not leave it silent and idle; instead give it the following prayer, "Lord Jesus Christ, Son of God, have mercy upon me."[5]

This last directive refers to the Jesus Prayer, or the Prayer of the Heart, to which we shall refer later.

Let the Spirit In

Breath is a very important word in the Old and New Testaments. The same word also means spirit ("ruach" in Hebrew, "pneuma" in Greek), and the connection between the two is a repeated theme in both testaments. Breath is also a symbol for life. In the Creation Story, it was only after God breathed upon the man whom he had formed from the dust of the earth that he became a living being. In Ezekiel's vision of the dry bones, he is commanded to prophesy that breath shall enter the bones, and they shall live. "Behold, I will cause breath (spirit) to enter you, and you shall live" (Ezek. 37:5). After his resurrection when he appeared to his disciples, Jesus followed the same ancient tradition of associating breath with creation in that he gave the Holy Spirit (Breath) to his disciples. "And when he had said this, he breathed ["pneuma" as a verb] on them, and said to them, 'Receive the Holy Spirit ["pneuma" as a noun]' " (John 20:22).

The connection of the Holy Spirit with a new creation is the basis for the celebrated experience of being "born again." The biblical description of new birth is located in the story of Jesus' encounter with the Pharisee, Nicodemus. When Nicodemus came to Jesus for spiritual enlightenment, Jesus told him it was necessary that he be born again. Confused about what this meant, Nicodemus asked whether he had to reenter his mother's womb. After a mild rebuke for his stupidity, Jesus described new birth as being born of the Spirit and used the analogy of the wind, which in Greek is the same word as that for breath and spirit. "The wind ["pneuma," n.] blows ["pneuma," vb.] where it wills, and you know the sound of it, but you do not know whence it comes or whither it goes; so it is with every one who is born of the spirit ["pneuma"]' (John 3:8).

We find the use of wind as an analogy for spirit in a description of the coming of the Holy Spirit at the Feast of Pentecost: While the disciples of Jesus were all gathered together in one place, "a sound came from heaven like the rush of a mighty wind, and it filled all the house where they were sitting. And they were all filled with the Holy Spirit" (Acts 2:2, 4).

A psychiatrist friend initiated me into meditation with an exercise of counting my breaths. I was to breathe deeply, feel the breath going in and out, and count my breaths, hoping to reach fifty before my mind wandered. If my mind wandered prior to fifty I either began again with the number I last recalled or began all over. As I practiced this exercise, I concentrated on feeling the expansion of my lungs as air (oxygen) entered, and the compression of my lungs as air (carbon dioxide) went out. I became aware of the moment of stillness after each exhalation prior to the tension that moves one automatically to inhale again. As I breathed in and out I also began to think of breath as spirit and imagined I was breathing in Holy Breath with the oxygen and breathing out poisonous spirits along with the carbon dioxide. As we receive the Spirit of God, spirits opposed to God must leave. Take in oxygen, breathe out carbon dioxide; take in the Holy Spirit, breathe out the divisive and obstructive spirits.

When we are tense our breathing is often irregular and shallow. We breathe up and down from our chest cavity rather than in and out from our diaphragm. This disruption in our breathing rhythm can disturb the harmony of other bodily functions. In the meditation exercise that we are about to begin, we will change this pattern by breathing regularly and deeply from the diaphragm. There is a rhythm to our breathing which we disrupt when we are under stress. In meditation we recapture this bodily rhythm and experience its relaxing effect on our minds and spirits as well as on our bodies. Focusing on the rhythm of deep breathing assists us in becoming still—open, trusting, comforted—so that we can know who is God. "Be still, and know that I am God" (Ps. 46:10).

Let the Spirit In

There are other consequences of deep breathing beyond relaxation and calmness. Studies have revealed that deep breathing is good for blood pressure, circulation, and the heart. In one such study the blood pressure of those who participated in deep breathing dropped after the exercise and continued so for thirty minutes. A deep breathing exercise program for a group of post-surgery hospital patients showed results that indicated a significant increase in blood circulation during the exercises. Another study has shown that pains from the heart condition of angina pectoris can be relieved by deep breathing. Still another indicates that those who regularly practice deep breathing have improved vital capacities—the volume of air one can forcefully exhale after inhalation—and still another has shown that those with good vital capacities are less inclined toward heart attacks. Regular physical exercise like running forces one to breathe deeply, and people with heart conditions are being encouraged to initiate walking and even running programs under their physician's guidance. Deep breathing in meditation can be helpful in effecting similar results and is a good supplement to a disciplined program of physical exercise.[6]

We are ready now to undertake a short deep breathing exercise. If you are reading this book in a study group, you will have the advantage of a support group in this endeavor. If you are alone, you will have to depend on your own initiative. Begin by placing yourself in a sitting position with both feet on the floor and your hands resting on your thighs. Breathe deeply from your abdomen. Once into the exercise you will concentrate on feeling your breath coming in as your lungs expand and going out as your lungs contract, feeling also the peaceful interlude that follows prior to the next inhalation. Focus on your abdomen in this moment of stillness. After a couple of minutes shift your focus from breath to the Holy Breath by thinking of yourself as taking in the Spirit of God with each inhalation and breathing out the divisive and obstructive spirits within you. I find it helpful to shut my eyes to environmental distractions for this focusing. We will pause now for a few minutes while you try this exercise. Wait until you have completed the exercise before reading the next paragraph.

Our next focus is on the abdomen. To us Westerners it may seem odd to select the abdomen as a meditational focus. Did it strike you as strange that the jogging guru directed healing to his stubbed toe from his abdomen? Actually, he was conditioned to do so by his exposure to Buddhist meditational practices. This focus on the abdomen, though Eastern, is also Christian. The abdomen is a very significant word in the New Testament although other words have been substituted for it in many of our modern translations. The abdomen—or the intestines or the bowels—is a bodily symbol for the human capacity for affection and compassion. The Greek word is "splagna." The King James Version translates it as bowels, sometimes coupling it with the attribute it symbolizes, such as compassion or mercy. An example is I John 3:17: "But whoso hath this world's goods, and seeth his brother have need, and shutteth up his bowels of compassion from him, how dwelleth the love of God in him?" The Revised Standard Version in this instance as in several others, translates "splagna" as heart, even though the Greek word for heart is "kardia." "But if any one has the world's goods and sees his brother in need, yet closes his heart against him, how does God's love abide in him?" While the heart is within the visceral area—its choice over intestines or bowels westernizes the translation.

Sometimes the Revised Standard Version (as does the New English Bible) completely eliminates the physical orientation of the word and translates it simply as affection. In Phil. 1:8, for example, St. Paul says, "For God is my witness, how I yearn for you with the affection of Jesus Christ." The word is literally with the intestines of Jesus Christ. The King James Version translates it as "the bowels of Jesus Christ." As the symbolic seat of our affection, compassion, and mercy, the abdominal region should occupy a significant role in Christian meditation.

Another problem we may have with the abdomen is that in contrast to the lungs, no movement—no breathing—is associated with it. How do you focus on that which seems stationary? The word "seems" was deliberately chosen because beneath the stationary exterior there is plenty of action, although we are not aware of it unless we have indigestion or other disturbances of our gastrointestinal tract. This tract is the place of our digestive activity—the source for the manufacture of bodily energy. Its choice as a biblical symbol for the energy of affection and compassion is thus not without physiological significance.

Deep breathing, as we have seen, begins and ends with the abdomen. In the meditative focus on deep breathing, we centered the moment of peace between breaths on the abdomen. One can feel all sorts of good feelings in this area of the body: warmth, pleasure, comfort. By the same token when we are under stress and tension, we often feel it in our abdomen in the form of indigestion, cramping, rumblings, and all the other symptoms that go with an "upset" or nervous stomach. By bringing relaxation and calm to body, mind, and spirit, the experience of meditation may counteract the physiological disturbances of the abdominal cavity that cause discomfort. There is good reason, therefore, to focus on the abdomen in meditation as a source of pleasure, warmth, and comfort. When digestion is functioning harmoniously, we feel good in our abdominal region.

The martial art of Ai-ki-do in which the Japanese excel, looks like a thoroughly physical skill. However, the secret to Ai-ki-do is mental concentration on the abdomen. The abdominal region is supposedly our body's center. Focusing on it while engaged in combat is focusing on our center of gravity. In a brief exposure to Ai-ki-do in a Human Potential seminar, I was amazed at how focusing my mind on my abdomen rooted me to the ground. If I took my mental focus off my abdomen, my opponent easily dislodged me from my position. One cannot be pulled or pushed "off one's feet" nearly so easily when one's mind is concentrating on one's abdominal region. It is as though the mind was reenforcing the pull of gravity to keep us fixed to the earth.

As the center of our body, the abdominal region can also serve as a symbol of our spiritual center—the basis for our personal stability and security. Centering is an old and familiar term in meditative practice. It means focusing on the source of our being. Our spiritual center is our relationship with God in whose image we are created. The Judeo-Christian understanding of man as created in God's image is relational in nature, that is, man is man only as he is in relationship or communion with the One who created him. The fall of man into sin is a falling out of relationship—with God, with himself, with his neighbor. The gospel of reconciliation restores us to relationship with God—and with ourself and our neighbor. To focus on our relationship with God involves maintaining an attitude of trust.

Focusing our mind on our security in relationship with God—or "rooted and grounded in love" as St. Paul described it—helps us keep our stability in inner conflicts just as focusing on our abdomen keeps us stable in martial arts. In both cases we are centering—in one on our mind, and in the other on our body—because the physical organ as well as the mental experience serves as a symbol of the spirit.

In addition to its being the source of good feelings and our

Let the Spirit In

physical center, the abdomen is also the region of energy production. In meditation this energy from the abdomen is often conceived of as "healing energy," as illustrated by what the jogging guru did for his stubbed toe. There is good reason for such symbolic conceptions. The energy released by digestion strengthens our body for its functioning, and in particular, strengthens our body for disease-resisting functions. Our disease-resisting cells are part of our physical endowment, but they need to be energized to fulfill their function. In the Lord's Supper, the function of eating and drinking necessary for physical energy is utilized symbolically in the reception of spiritual food. The gospel of reconciliation that unites us with God is mediated through the death and resurrection of Jesus Christ. His body and his blood are the elements of our reconciliation and spiritual security. They are "received" by mouth in the Lord's Supper under the symbols of bread and wine—food and drink.

We are ready now for the second initiating exercise into meditation. Begin again with deep breathing, focusing on the abdomen during the quiet moment between breaths. After a minute or so shift your focus entirely to your abdomen. First attempt to "pick up" how it "feels." If your digestion is working well, you may sense the pleasantness of the abdominal region, its warmth, its comfort. Secondly, focus on your abdomen as the center of your body. Let it become a symbol to you of your personal center—your security with God. Consider yourself stabilized by this focus. Thirdly, focus on your abdomen as a source of energy—healing energy—going throughout your body and also into your mind and spirit. You may even wish to direct it to particular places or needs where healing is desired. We will pause now for you to do this exercise for a few minutes. Again wait until you have completed the exercise before reading the next paragraph.

3. *Listening to Our Bodies*

The meditational focus on breathing and the abdomen is a way of listening to our bodies. This sort of listening does not come naturally in our work-and-project-oriented culture. We treat our bodies like we do the rest of nature. Obtaining unwarranted license from the biblical directive to "subdue" nature, we dominate, misuse, and exploit it. As a result we have an environmental crisis on our hands. In like manner we exploit our bodies as means to our achievements: we drive them, abuse them, but rarely listen to them, until they cry out in pain. Even then we may ignore them under the illusion that to ignore pain shows strength and courage. We have become alienated from our bodies and so have little rapport with them: they have taken a beating figuratively if not literally from our life-styles, priorities, and pursuits—all of which are highly influenced by a society in which nature is viewed as something to be mastered.

So if you felt a bit awkward in these exercises you have good reason; it is not the sort of thing to which you have been inclined by our cultural values. You may have felt even more strange when you used the body and its functions as a symbol or analogy of the functions of the spirit. The ancient perspective of the physical as unrelated or even in opposition to the spirit is still with us, at least in our feelings.

These initiatory exercises provide a needed balance for us in relating to our own humanness. I would encourage you to continue with them until the strangeness wears off and you begin to enjoy the experience.

The rather recent practice of biofeedback is a form of listening to our bodies. Using machines one can "monitor" one's bodily functions and through mental focus attempt to alter them. In this way some people have learned to reduce their tensions and pains without the use of drugs—or even when drugs have had a diminishing effect. In achieving some control over functions largely governed by the autonomic nervous system, they have accomplished what Western medicine had assumed was beyond voluntary control. In the Eastern world the idea of such control was not only accepted, but cultivated. In biofeedback we have the Eastern discipline of mental control over bodily functions coupled with Western technology as an example of how the two cultures may complement each other. The machine assists us to listen to our bodies, and as we learn to listen, we can learn also to direct.

4. Meditating in the Rhythm of Movement

While learning the process of meditation, it is probably best to meditate in a stationary position, preferably seated in a straight chair. After you become more accustomed to the process, you may also want to meditate when your body is in movement. The most obvious way is to meditate while walking. The rhythm of walking fits naturally with the rhythm of deep breathing. When the Old Testament patriarch Isaac was waiting for the caravan bringing a wife to him from the land of his father Abraham, he "went out to meditate in the fields in the evening" (Gen. 24:63). The translation of this sentence is difficult because the meaning of the Hebrew word here translated as "meditate" is unknown to us. The word could also be simply understood as taking a stroll or even relieving oneself. In spite of the obscurity of the text, it is possible to consider this patriarch of the Judeo-Christian heritage confronting his anxiety over the approaching caravan by taking a meditative walk in the fields at the close of the day. At least the translators of several important versions decided in this direction.

Walking to work or to other places rather than driving our car is a wise expenditure of time as well as a conservation of oil. If we are concerned about the quality of our lives as well as the quantity of our achievements, we may have to contemplate a change of life-style. Walking will slow us down, but that may not be bad—even quantitatively. A nonagenarian who had been and still is a vigorous hiker said, "I hike to live, and I love living." A noted psychiatrist has said that a five-mile hike is good therapy for almost any emotional disturbance. I agree with him. Meditating while walking adds to the pleasure and value of each.

Another combination is meditating while running. Since Glasser has concluded that running and meditating are the two chief ways to positive addiction, one can put them together and have the best of all worlds. Obviously a caution is needed. One needs to be in condition to run. A physical examination should indicate whether running is for you or not. If it is, begin with short distances and add to these gradually. Run every other day to allow the muscles and joints a rest. Only after you have your running stride—and this may take a year or more—should you attempt to meditate while running. When you are sufficiently freed from the strain of the effort, you will be able to give your mind to other things. It is important to follow a familiar running track while meditating. As your body runs in rhythm you can let your mind and spirit go on their own. The YMCA slogan, "Run for Your Life," stresses the value of running for your health, once you are in condition. Age is no insurmountable barrier and even some with heart problems who are under their physicians' guidance are running for their lives.

Chapter Three

MEDITATION AND THE USE OF THE IMAGINATION

As you are aware by now, meditation, among other things, is an exercise of the imagination. Dr. Harold Greenwald of Direct Decision Therapy refers to meditation simply as "focused imagination." His approach, like Glasser's, gives little significance to the spiritual or the religious in human functioning. Meditation makes positive use of the imagination which is a very powerful human faculty. We seem to be aware of this power mostly when it is used negatively. In moments of anxiety we say that we "let our imagination run away with us," or in any tense situation when the future is unknown we tend to "imagine the worst."

1. A Positive Use of a Powerful Faculty

The classic story from the Bible concerning this negative use of the imagination is that of the Israelites' panic at the entrance to the Promised Land. They had been delivered from their enslavement in Egypt for the expressed purpose of returning to the land of Canaan. They endured much hardship and deprivation in their journey to that land. When they arrived, however, their fear became stronger than their anticipation.

Twelve men were sent to spy out the land. When they returned, ten of these reflected the fears of the people. They described the land as one that "devours its inhabitants. All of the people in it are of great stature," and in comparison to these giants, they saw themselves "like grasshoppers."

The other two spies, Caleb and Joshua, tried to deflate these images: "Let us go up at once," they said, "for we are well able to occupy it." But all the people could "see" were giants—and they refused to enter. Their fear had immobilized them at their moment of destiny. So they wandered in the wilderness for forty years until a new generation emerged that had the courage to enter under Joshua's leadership.

The writer of the New Testament Epistle to the Hebrews sees universal meaning in this story. Each person under God has the opportunity to break out of the slavery of old patterns and enter into the freedom of the new. Therefore he says, "Today, when you hear his voice, do not harden your hearts as in the rebellion" (3:15). In Christ he sees one who like Joshua can lead people into the promised land, but the "land" is a spiritual state he calls "rest." "Let us therefore strive to enter that rest, that no one fall by the same sort of disobedience" (4:11).

It is tragic when people permit their imagination to fortify their fears so that they wander in the wilderness—in circles of futility—when they could have gone forward to claim God's promises. They fear failure and imagine themselves failing. They fear illness and imagine themselves coming down with disease. They fear competition and imagine themselves as defeated. Because they see themselves as "grasshoppers," the competitors are "giants." The giants become enemies determined to crush the grasshoppers. The picture they "see" is paranoid—which literally means beyond the mind or reason. It becomes the center of an imagination "gone bananas" with fear. The power behind our self-fulfilling prophecies is that we are linked to the negative picture we have of ourselves in our imagination.

In meditation we reverse this disintegrating process by joining our imagination to the power of faith. We connect it

Let the Spirit In

with God's promises rather than with our fears. We use it for positive programming rather than negative programming.

Secular meditation frequently refers to this activity as "fantasizing." Fantasizing and imagining are much the same, except that fantasy implies a departure from reality. Both activities are based on our mind's ability to make pictures—to direct its own journey into "picture-land." Imagining is really "image-ing."

Image-ing is at the heart of Jesus' method of teaching. In fact, according to the Gospels, he taught nothing to people except by parable. A parable is a story that communicates a truth. Stories stimulate the imagination because we visualize word-images in our minds as we hear them. And we perceive the truth because we literally see it!

Some of Jesus' parables are powerful stimuli to the imagination, but so are the truths that they illustrate. As an example, take what seems to be his favorite analogy—that of the mustard seed. He uses it to describe both the Kingdom of God and the power of faith. The mustard seed is the smallest of seeds and yet when it is sown it grows into a shrub large enough for birds to build their nests in its branches. Who could expect such a little thing to be capable of so much? So the truth is that if you have faith as a grain of mustard seed, you might say to a sycamine tree—or even to a mountain—be rooted up and be planted—or be cast into the sea—and it would obey you (Luke 17:6; Matt. 21:21). Can you see the tree impelled out of the soil and hurtling into the sea! The affective idea that comes through so vividly in these action pictures is that of power—not simply power as an abstract idea, but a power in which we can participate. The dynamic image of the parable inspires (breathes into) us to believe.

In meditation we direct our imagination in precisely these ways. We picture our possibilities and our hopes as ventures in faith. We are inspired by the parable of the mustard seed to

Meditation and the Use of the Imagination   ◁ *39*

let our imagination go in the direction of faith. We use parables as pictures that assist us to concretize—to "see." In the meditative state we lay "tracks" in our mind by using our imagination. Meditation is a "conditioning" exercise that influences us to follow these tracks in the real life situations to which they are related.

2. A Form of Prayer

If we think of meditation not simply as a mental or spiritual exercise but also as a devotional exercise, then directing our imagination in meditation can be thought of as a form of prayer. A collect that I frequently use when concluding a meditation contains the petition, "Lord grant us . . . thoughts that pass into prayers." Our thoughts frequently take the form of mental pictures. They "pass into prayers" when we direct these pictures to God. When we use words in our prayers, it is not so that God can hear or understand, rather our use of words is for our own clarification. Words sharpen our awareness. The conscious directing of our mental images as petitions to God is prayer without words. It is a form of prayer that fits quite naturally into a meditative situation in which one's activity is deeply focused. In devotional meditation the directed use of the imagination has a "relational" dimension. One is not simply communing with oneself, but also with God. God is everywhere present, and even through prayer his presence is not something we direct or manipulate. "Lo, I am with you always" (Matt. 28:20). Our "awareness" of his presence, however, is something else. Devotional meditation is a focusing on this awareness, and directing our imagination in relationship to this awareness is a way of petitioning God.

Suppose you are facing a challenge in the near future—such as attempting to persuade a decision-making

Let the Spirit In

body to adopt a particular course of action. As the appointed time approaches your doubts may increase. You are not sure you will be able to think clearly or speak effectively—you imagine that your emotions will get the better of you. As your anxiety begins to feed your imagination, your doubts may become actual mental images of failure. In devotional meditation you can reverse the buildup of anxiety by guiding your imagination in the opposite direction—by "seeing" yourself in action before the group, functioning with clarity of thought, effectiveness of speech, and with feelings of confidence rather than fear or anger. Since your meditation is oriented to the presence of God, your new image of a confident performance is your petition to God to help you in the challenge.

The usual way of praying is to petition God in words as we would another person. I certainly do not wish to detract from this way of praying. I use it myself. According to Jesus, what is important to prayer is that we pray in faith. It is possible to pray with positive words and yet retain an attitude of doubt. When we pray by directing our imagination to visualize that for which we are praying, we have already taken a step—often called a leap—in the direction of faith. I once asked a very religious mother who prayed regularly for her rebellious daughter if she could imagine her daughter with an attitude of confidence and faith. She shook her head as if she were confronted with an ironic impossibility. The thought-picture of a rebellious daughter was overwhelming. "All I can see," she said, "is that sullen face!" How then could she pray in the face of this overpowering obstacle to her imagination?

It takes courage to envision a change when we honestly face the negative. It is the "leap of faith" that breaks new ground—at least in the imagination. We can become so accustomed to our negative mind-set that a prayer of faith

Meditation and the Use of the Imagination   ◁ 41

seems to belong to the world of fantasy. Actually this meditative use of the imagination opens us to a reality that is beyond our impression of reality. Because we tend to identify reality with our interpretation of it, we are taking steps in faith when we exercise our imagination beyond a static interpretation.

Does it take a major effort on your part to picture your problems in a manner that permits, or even encourages, a positive resolution? If so, your prayer of faith begins here as you dare to imagine what God can do in and with any situation. The leap of faith is not just any leap, but a leap in the direction of God's promises. It is a leap in faith because we do not know for sure where we will land. There is a risk in taking the leap and there are no guarantees. Our imagination is capable of picturing our hopes, but it needs direction. When we take charge of our imagination, it is at this point that we begin the venture of faith. It is a first response to the presence of God. In giving this response we are opening the way for God to work in our lives as well as supporting his influence in the lives of others.

3. Prayers of Intercession

There was a time when those who considered themselves sophisticated would scoff at the idea that one can influence another by prayer, but in our day one does not have to be religious to take the idea seriously. Human potentialists speak of sending "energy" to one another. Physicians and psychiatrists talk about the value of a support group—people who covenant together to care for one another. Some of the most significant of these are prayer groups. Although we do not know how intercessory prayer influences others, suppose that the theory that we "send" telepathiclike messages or "energy" to another person by projecting our imagination were true. The Silva Mind Control program which claims to be based on a "science of the mind," suggests that we have the potential for extrasensory capacities that can be developed through conditioning exercises; that is we can be sensitized to "pick up" the mental imagery another may be directing toward us, and also direct our own positive imagery toward others to influence healing in their own diseased bodies or minds. For this reason the conditioning ritual of the Silva program contains a repeated commitment to use these "powers" for constructive purposes only.

If you feel that theory about how intercessory prayer "works" displaces God you have good reason. Our religious training has often associated God's actions with miracles or other inexplicable phenomena. Consequently, if in our growing scientific knowledge we can describe the processes by which some of these heretofore inexplicable phenomena occur, what happens then to God? Associating God with the inexplicable is one of the causes for the supposed conflict between science and religion which still goes on at a subdued level. The problem with this understanding of God's ways, as Dietrich Bonhoeffer has pointed out, is that it reserves God for the gaps in our knowledge. Should the gaps be filled, God is then "eliminated." But even worse, reserving God for the gaps "eliminates" him from a great portion of our everyday life.

This problem arises when we make an unfortunate division in our minds between a natural and supernatural order. God's involvement in life then becomes an intervention from another realm. But according to the Judeo-Christian tradition, God is the creator and sustainer of the natural order. He has not withdrawn from it even though that order is fallen. He is present in the world and is working through the natural order. God works through his creation—through means. If we

Meditation and the Use of the Imagination   ◁ 43

discover how God's creation operates, could this possibly "reduce" God's role? He is the One who creates "out of nothing." We work within his creation to achieve the possibilities inherent in it.

As we apply this understanding of God and his creation to the subject of intercessory prayer, we need see no threat to God or to prayer even if a theory about the projected energy of the mind could be substantiated. We do have clinical evidence concerning the therapeutic results of support groups. Consequently, we develop theories about how such therapy operates. But we still have only theories. Also, support groups are only one factor among others in healing, and by themselves can offer no guarantees.

We pray for others for many reasons: we care about them; we believe in God; we want to see change take place in their lives. From a Christian point of view there is another reason: the revelation we have of God in the Bible clearly affirms that God wants us to pray for ourselves and for others. He chooses to work with us in this way. Our prayers are actually in response to his overtures. It is not that we are trying to convince him by our prayers; rather, through prayer he is encouraging our participation in a partnership of concern.

In our intercessory prayers we are supporting others by using a means of positively influencing them. In meditational intercession we use our imagination to picture people receiving that which they need. If a person is ill, we picture him or her becoming well. If he or she is lacking purpose or meaning—a sense of calling—we picture him or her as receiving that meaning, giving meaning a visual symbol such as a confident countenance. In this form of prayer, the choice of symbols in communicating our intercession may be meaningful only to ourselves, but it is this meaning that is sent—communicated—with the symbol.

4. Meditational Exercise

We are now ready for our next initiatory exercise in meditation. We will begin as before with deep breathing and its analogy to Spirit and the abdominal focus symbolizing comfort, security, and healing energy. After spending a few minutes in this preparatory exercise, direct your imagination into forming petitions of prayer for yourself and others. For this exercise select something concerning yourself for which you seek God's help and select another person whom you believe needs your intercession. If you are in a study group, I suggest that you select someone in need who is known to all of you and focus on this person together in your intercession. Use your imagination as vividly as possible in shaping mental pictures and symbols. Again, wait until you have completed this exercise before reading the next paragraph.

5. Imagery and Healing

Recently I observed Agnes Sanford, long associated with the ministry of healing, as she responded to requests from persons in her audience for prayers for healing. She followed the ritual that I had anticipated: she questioned each individual about his or her particular need, placed one hand on his or her shoulder and the other across the forehead in the laying on of hands, and prayed specifically for healing. But she did more that I had not anticipated. I was impressed by her dialogue with each individual. She drew out not only the nature of the particular ailment, but also the person's feelings regarding it and his or her degree of desire and openness for healing. After obtaining a specific understanding of the person and his or her illness, she chose specific imagery to visualize the illness and counterimagery to describe the process of healing. She used these images in her prayer, and as she asked God to heal the disease, she pictured the process as though it were taking place. After the prayer she encouraged the person to continue praying in this manner and to anticipate healing, not necessarily immediately, but gradually.

This use of imagery in a meditative state as it pertains to the working of our body processes is being used increasingly as an aid to the healing process. I have referred previously to Dr. Carl Simonton who uses this procedure as an assist to the treatment of cancer. Alpha-Dynamics and other forms of self-hypnosis prescribe a meditative ritual for the relief of headaches, including migraine. Through the use of the imagination one directs the pain to leave believing that it will. Imagining specific colors adds to the vividness and character of the imagery. Red, for example, may symbolize inflammation, while yellow may symbolize healing. By making the imagery as clear and personal as possible, we are providing a means for the mind to direct the body.

In devotional meditation our position is that of creature. We do not function as autonomous persons, but as persons under God. Our meditation is a relational experience with another. We may use means also common to other groups who differ from us in terms of religious faith, but this does not mean that we are each doing the same thing. The position of creature under God constitutes a radical difference since one's entire perspective is shaped by it. A wholly different dimension of life is involved. Working through his created order God uses means—the potentials of his own creation—to accomplish his ends. So also in our role as creatures we too use means (e.g., images), but as "fellow workers" with the creator and not apart from him. We are fulfilled as persons in spirit as well as in mind through our relationship with God.

Chapter Four

MEDITATION AND PRAYER

Devotional meditation is meditation with the perspective of faith in God. It is therefore organically related to prayer. This relationship was developed to some extent in the previous chapter when the imagination was used in meditation to form pictorial petitions in the presence of God. In this chapter we shall describe further the relationship of meditation to prayer and the place of prayer in devotional meditation.

1. *Prayer as Differentiated from Meditation*

How shall we differentiate meditation from prayer? Archbishop Anthony Bloom, Russian Orthodox prelate in exile and contemporary writer on meditation and prayer, says meditation is preparation for prayer. "Meditation primarily means thinking, even when God is the object of our thoughts." As we become increasingly aware of the presence of God, meditation gradually moves into prayer. However, there is no mutuality, for prayer should not "degenerate" into meditation.[7]

Bloom's categories are obviously different from mine. For him, meditation includes Bible study, while I separate Bible study from meditation, even though I use the Bible in meditation as we shall see in the next chapter. According to Bloom, prayer uses words, but he emphasizes that words themselves do not constitute the prayer. For Bloom prayer is essentially giving God our undivided attention in the consciousness of his presence. While I believe that much of our prayer uses words, I also believe that a specific kind of meditative prayer uses mind pictures. The very word combination, "meditative prayer," would be impossible in Bloom's categories. In devotional meditation as I define it, meditation can be distinguished from prayer but not separated from it since the two may come together in meditative prayer. "Thoughts that pass into prayers" do not cease being thoughts, but rather are thoughts or mental images directed toward God. Bloom's categories, though mystical and Eastern Orthodox in content and structure, are essentially those of daily devotions, namely, Bible study and prayer.

A similar differentiation of meditation from prayer was made by an instructor in TM. Although the reason for his differentiation was based on the same radical distinction between prayer and meditation, TM's understanding of meditation is quite different from that of Bloom. TM is not content-oriented; it is not thought; rather, it is the suspension of thought. To achieve this suspension one is given a "mantra"—a word with no meaning—upon which to focus. Buddhist meditation aims at this same suspension of the reasoning mind. Instead of a mantra, the learner in the Rinzai School of Zen Buddhism is given a "koan" which is a riddle or paradox. However it is not the usual riddle since the answer to the koan is not the product of reason or logic. In fact, meditating upon the koan is in defiance of reason. The meditator puts aside all rational thoughts and lets fantasy, whim, and nonsense reign. An example: "What is the sound of one hand clapping?"

The relationship between this kind of meditation and prayer, according to the TM instructor, is that the former may lead to the latter. "Religious people," he said (the implication was Christian religious people), "use Transcendental Meditation as preparation for prayer." In decelerating the usual mental activity, meditation would predispose one to be more receptive to the activity of prayer.

In my conception of devotional meditation, meditation is a disciplined focus of thought which slows the often frenetic pace of our minds so that we become more open to the Spirit. However, the focus is not just upon any thoughts, but rather upon those thoughts conducive to prayer. Meditation assists us to achieve that condition of spirit described by Isaiah: "In returning and rest you shall be saved; in quietness and in trust shall be your strength" (30:15). The readiness with which the meditational focus can enter into visualized petition shows that there are no rigid boundaries between meditation and prayer unless one so defines each to insure such boundaries. A response of gratitude and thanksgiving (to the reception of peace and quietness, for example) is implicit in a devotional perspective. There is Someone to thank.

2. Sanctuaries for Meditation

It is ironic that, according to Adam Smith, meditators who use TM in a secular form discover that churches are the best place to meditate. As Smith puts it, they are the only places open in midcity that respect silence, other than the public library. In addition to respecting silence, church sanctuaries are designed to assist in meditation and prayer. The architecture is symbolic, encouraging a meditative mood with the perspective of faith in God. The arches point heavenward. The stained glass windows and other artwork depict biblical stories and symbols. So it is no coincidence that the place meditators find most appropriate in the city is a worship sanctuary designed for this purpose.

From its beginnings the Judeo-Christian tradition has

placed high priority on the place of worship. In the Old Testament period while the Israelites were still enroute to their promised homeland, they erected a tent which not only provided a place for worship, but which symbolized the presence of God in their midst. Later King David's ambition to build a temple as "God's dwelling place" was realized by his son Solomon whose temple was one of the marvels of the ancient world. After it was destroyed by the conquering Babylonians, the returning exiles rebuilt it at the cost of much sacrifice.

In the Christian era, the emphasis on place of worship continued, ranging from small house churches to magnificent cathedrals. The church edifice is often referred to as the "house of God." Says Bloom, "When we come to Church we should be aware that we are entering upon sacred ground."[8] When the creature enters the "house of his Creator," he is encouraged by the atmosphere, the mystique, and the architecture to respond in a creaturely way. Consequently, meditation in a Christian sense is, by its very context, devotional. And whether engaged in while walking, in one's room, in a public conveyance, or in a church, the atmosphere of a sanctuary is still present within one.

In addition to the sanctuaries of churches providing a meditative setting, there are also sanctuaries of nature. The appeal of nature to our spiritual sensitivities has inspired both prophets and poets. "The heavens," says the psalmist, "declare the glory of God; and the firmament sheweth his handiwork. . . . There is no speech nor language, where their voice is not heard" (Ps. 19: 1, 3 KJV). Hills, valleys, mountains, woods, lakes, rivers, streams, and even deserts provide an ambience that draws from us a sense of awe. We feel a kinship with nature and an adoration for its creator. Mountains seem to be especially significant. Grandiose and peaked, they not only point as nature's arches to the heavens,

Let the Spirit In

but also make us feel small in an aesthetic rather than a melancholy way. We experience our creatureliness within an awareness of the Transcendent One who transcends all limits.

The sanctuaries of nature were often used by Jesus as places for meditation and prayer as an alternative to the temple and synagogue which he also frequented. He chose the desert to battle with temptation, the mountains for prayer, the garden for meditation and decision-making, and the "lonely places" for times of retreat. The experience of his transfiguration took place on a mountaintop to which he and his three close disciples had climbed as the climax of a planned retreat. "[He] led them up a high mountain apart by themselves" (Mark 9:2). Although the mountain is not named in the Gospel accounts, it was thought among early Christians to have been Mt. Tabor, a mountain significant in Old Testament history as the place during the period of the Judges where Barak gathered his troops to resist the oppression of the Assyrians. On this mountain Jesus was transfigured, that is, "his garments became glistening, intensely white, as no fuller on earth could bleach them" (Mark 9:3). It was a "mountain-top" experience for Jesus and his disciples, as the term has since come to mean. When Abraham Maslow chose the term "peak experience" to describe the religious or mystical experiences that he observed were characteristic of healthy-minded people, he was using a description with a long Christian tradition.

Far different, but no less religious, was the experience of Jesus and his disciples in the Garden of Gethsemane. Again he chose a place where he could wrestle with temptation, this time to reaffirm the identity he had received on Mt. Tabor. The night prior to his crucifixion he left the upper room with his disciples troubled in spirit by what he knew was about to happen. Judas had already left the group to arrange the betrayal. Even though it was dark, Jesus needed the sanctuary of the garden, for he had come there often to pray. He wanted the appropriate atmosphere in which to deal with his anguish and to prepare himself for his ordeal. Instead of being transfigured, however, he perspired with bloody sweat and asked God that he be spared from the cross using the familiar symbol of the "bitter cup" (see Luke 22:42-44). But he emerged from his spiritual struggle in this sanctuary ready to drink from that cup as an affirmation of his mission.

3. Jesus as a Model

We can learn a great deal from the devotional habits of Jesus. Christians have always looked to Jesus as a model and have been encouraged to walk "in his steps." Normally we are encouraged to follow him in our behavior toward others, yet I have rarely heard any encouragement to follow him in his life of meditation and prayer. Can you imagine someone saying that he or she planned to climb a mountain for a place to pray? If there are people who do this, they would probably be reluctant to say so. One climbs a mountain in our Western culture for the view or the exercise or the aesthetic satisfaction or the physical exhilaration or the sport, but to climb a mountain or hike in the woods or enter a garden to pray would be rather unusual to say the least.

It was not only the effort that Jesus put into securing the right place for prayer that seems foreign, but also the time that he put into it. "And in the morning, a great while before day, he rose and went out to a lonely place, and there he prayed" (Mark 1:35). Many of his followers have found that the morning hours are freest from distraction and fatigue to engage in prayer, besides being a good way to begin a day. But Jesus did not confine himself to mornings. "In those days he went to the mountain to pray; and all night he continued in prayer to God" (Luke 6:12). How can one be ready for the day without having slept? Evidently he received the refreshment normally supplied by sleep from prayer. I doubt that we should understand prayer in this instance as continuous conversation with God. When persons in intimate relationships spend a considerable amount of time together, they seldom feel the necessity to keep talking. They may instead enjoy the relationship in quietness. On this occasion, Jesus chose to spend the night in conscious communion with God. It is quite likely that this included meditation as well as prayer.

Should you have trouble sleeping on any particular occasion, try devoting this time to conscious communion with God. You will not feel as dragged out the next day, and you may actually enjoy the experience. It is certainly an improvement over the usual frustration of "trying" to get to sleep. The security that comes from intimacy is quite different from the dreaded loneliness that one often feels at these times. In fact, it is so pleasant and restful you may, in spite of yourself, go to sleep.

While the Christianity that most of us know bears the impact of Western culture the fact is that our Judeo-Christian heritage has its origins in the Mideast. As a human being Jesus was an Easterner, and even today his devotional habits fit more with an Eastern than a Western life-style, for the East has not changed much in this respect. Consequently, we can learn something about meditation and prayer from Eastern churches who have been separated, and even estranged, from Western churches for almost a thousand years. Fortunately the recent ecumenical movement has brought the West and the East into the beginnings of a dialogue in which we can learn from each other the distinctive values of the way each has conceived of the Christian vocation.

Meditation and Prayer   ◁ 53

4. *Prayer of the Heart*

One of the results of this dialogue is a growing Western appreciation for the Hesychast tradition of the "prayer of the heart." The current meditative movement was in its early stages when Huston Smith suggested that Christendom could contribute to the growing fascination for Eastern meditation with the Jesus Prayer.[9] Christian writers on meditation, such as Bloom and Henry Nouwen, and even writers who are concerned with Eastern religious patterns, such as Naranjo and Robert Ornstein, have spoken positively in regard to the Jesus Prayer. The prayer is "Lord Jesus Christ, have mercy upon me," which many Christians will recognize as the "Kyrie eleison" (Lord, have mercy) which may be part of their own worship service.

The idea of the "prayer of the heart" is that such a prayer comes from one's heart or is habituated to one's heart. Nouwen defines it as "the prayer that is most our own and that forms a unique way of reaching out to God."[10] "The Way of the Pilgrim," a Hesychast classic which describes one person's search for the prayer of the heart, says that this prayer should be "a short one consisting of a few powerful words" which can be repeated many times. "The mind should be in the heart . . . guiding the heart while it prays."[11] For the Hesychasts, as illustrated by the Pilgrim in the book, the prayer of the heart is the "Kyrie," which meets the above requirements. "This prayer," said one of the early Hesychasts, "will teach you everything."

The Jesus Prayer contains much religious knowledge. In fact, some would say it contains the heart of the Gospel.[12] It describes Jesus as the Lord of our lives and as the Messiah (Christ) through whom we receive God's mercy (grace). As creatures we are dependent on his mercy. The prayer itself is an expression of the relationship of communion that his grace

Let the Spirit In

makes possible; it is an expression of our response to God's desire to give through our asking.

For Westerners at least, this prayer may seem incomplete; praying for mercy does not automatically imply that one has received it—or that one can pray for mercy only because one has already received it. The Good News is that God has had mercy upon us—even though we need continually to receive this mercy. In my own denominational worship the "Kyrie" is followed by the "Gloria," in which God is praised. A prayer of praise can also be a "prayer of the heart." We can praise God that in his mercy he has responded to our sorry condition by initiating the means to redeem us. His initiative has provided us with the needed security to enter into his presence. As the writer of the Epistle to the Hebrews puts it, "Let us then with confidence draw near to the throne of grace, that we may receive mercy and find grace to help in time of need" (4:16). In the "Kyrie" we are responding to Jesus' invitation to ask and by the power of his Spirit we are also receiving.

In the Hesychast tradition one meditates upon, prays, and otherwise "fills one's being" with the prayer of one's heart. By such meditative conditioning the prayer "enters the heart." As the Pilgrim expresses it, "I had the feeling that the Prayer had, so to speak, by its own action passed from my lips to my heart. . . . I gave up saying the Prayer with my lips. I listened carefully to what my heart was saying."[13] One is reminded of John Wesley's familiar words from the Aldersgate Street religious meeting which altered his life. "I felt my heart strangely warmed." Said the Pilgrim, "There came into my heart a gracious warmth which spread through my whole breast."[14] Through meditative conditioning, the Jesus Prayer had become the prayer of his heart and was now a part of him. In fact, as Nouwen points out, it is through such internalizing that we may realize that prayer is not simply something we do but something also that the Spirit of God does in us.[15] Cambridge Regius Professor of Divinity G. W. H. Lampe states it well: "Prayer is an activity of God himself, incarnated in the thoughts and aspirations and concerns of men and expressed in human language; at the same time it is man's own activity, prompted and guided and inspired of God."[16]

5. Praying with Words in Meditation

It should be evident by now that in the Christian tradition prayer is inseparable from meditation. Prayer is our response to the presence of God in the context of meditation. As is evident from the prayer of the heart, we may even meditate upon prayers. In the Eastern Orthodox tradition one is encouraged to concentrate on the words of a prayer. Not only the "Kyrie" but the Lord's Prayer can be used for this purpose. In line with Bloom's emphasis, one "pronounces the words of the prayer attentively." He quotes St. John Climacus as advocating the same procedure in learning to concentrate upon a chosen prayer as my psychiatrist friend recommended to me in learning to relax my body and my mind by counting my breaths. If your mind wanders during your word by word concentration on a chosen prayer, you restart the prayer on the word you last recall, even if you have to do so "fifty times."[17] In this way one develops the power of mental focus.

Words are very meaningful to prayer. When Jesus' disciples asked him to teach them to pray, for example, he taught them what we now call the Lord's Prayer—a prayer with seven petitions, carefully worded and in a definite progression. Whether or not you use a specificly formulated prayer of the heart in meditation, you need to feel free to express yourself spontaneously in prayer at any time—using words, thinking them only in your mind, whispering them with your lips, or audibly voicing them. In devotional meditation one is involved in an intimate relationship and spontaneity must not be ruled out for the sake of structure.

I have already directed you in an exercise of prayer in which words were replaced by mental pictures to convey meaning. Prayers may also be conveyed by means of words in devotional meditation. I have already referred to a petition from the following prayer that comes close to my prayer of the heart.

> Grant us, O Lord, for our growth, thoughts that pass into prayers, prayers that pass into love and love that passes into eternal life, through Jesus Christ our Lord. Amen.

As a conclusion to this chapter we will take another meditation exercise. Select a prayer, whether the Jesus Prayer, the Lord's Prayer (or specific petitions from it), the collect above, or another prayer that you like. After repeating the breathing focus and the abdominal focus, go through the prayer, taking each word, phrase, or specific petition and give it your total concentration—think it, feel it, direct it to God. You may discover new insights into its meaning for you. Begin the exercise now before turning to the next chapter.

Chapter Five
MEDITATION AND SCRIPTURE

1. *Scripture as Word of God*

In the Christian tradition the Bible is a basic resource for meditation, providing content for thought. This is in contrast to prevailing Eastern meditative forms which make a deliberate attempt to screen out thought content from the mind. Christianity, on the other hand, is characterized by a recurring tension between thought and feeling, or—to use the familiar symbols—between the head and the heart, with the head symbolizing the reasoning self and the heart symbolizing the intuitive or feeling self. Both head and heart are needed for knowledge and understanding. In devotional meditation the focus is on the head and the heart, with phrases like "thinking in the heart" or "getting the head into the heart," describing this balance.

I have heard Christian meditators say that they use the name, Jesus, as a mantra in their meditation, indicating their attempt to adapt TM to their own faith. While I am aware of their purpose, the name, Jesus, has serious limitations as a mantra because it has historical as well as emotional meaning in the life of the meditator, being literally loaded with rational (head) and emotional (heart) content. Although the nature of the mantra differs with different Eastern traditions of meditation, in TM the mantra is usually a word provided by the instructor as the pupil's own meditative word upon which to focus and is without prior meaning to the pupil. When we say the name Jesus, however, we are not referring just to a word but to a unique person in history, the incidents of whose life are familiar to the Christian community. He is the one through whose death and resurrection God has reconciled us to himself, to ourselves, and to other people. His name brings other symbols to mind—love, truth, Lord, Savior, Brother, Shepherd. We can make a good case for using the name Jesus as a contemplative focus for meditation, but not as a TM mantra whose minimal content assists one to suspend all thought. Contemplation—a prolonged mental focus on a meaningful symbol—is a familiar practice in Christian meditation with its rich store of religious symbols. Bernard of Clairvaux has expressed the significance of Jesus' name for Christians in poetry.

> Nor voice can sing, nor heart can frame,
> Nor can the memory find
> A sweeter sound than thy blest Name,
> O Saviour of mankind!

The difference between the focus of contemplation and the focus of TM on a mantra is an indication of the difference between TM and Christian forms of meditation.

2. Scripture as the Word of God

In the Christian context the Scripture is received as the Word of God. The Word of God, however, is not identical with the Bible. Jesus is called the Word—the Living Word—as is the Gospel. The Sacraments are sometimes referred to as the "Visible Word." Both Bible and Sacraments serve as means of grace, that is, as divinely designated ways of receiving the love and mercy of God. To distinguish the use of the Bible as the Word of God, the Scripture is frequently called the "Written Word."

As the Word of God, the Bible is also a resource for prayer. God speaks to us through his Word, and we respond to him through prayer. The contextual use of the Bible as a means of grace is relational. The Holy Spirit initiates communion with our spirits through the Word.

In devotional meditation we use the Scripture both as content for meditation and as a catalyst for communion. The content has a specific reference to our needs, desires, and responsibilities. The use of word pictures in the Bible—its stories and parables—stimulates the recipient to see as well as to hear. Old Testament prophets spoke of the "Word of God which I saw," almost as frequently as of "the Word of God which I heard." The New Testament verb to see (Greek, "orao") can also mean to experience or to know. Our usage is similar in English when we say, "I see," to mean, "I understand." The story or parable stimulates the imagination to see and thereby to understand; it illustrates or makes bright the point, and we are enlightened.

Using the Bible in meditation is not the same as studying it. We need to study the Bible to secure our resources from it for meditation, but to study is not "ipso facto" to meditate. As the word study implies, Bible study is primarily a rational activity. While reasoning is operative in devotional meditation, the process is different than in studying. Terms like "deeper level of consciousness" are used to describe the difference. The scope of mental activity is limited and the pace is slowed. The purpose is to see and hear and know. Heart as well as head are included in the focus. The content of the Word we select for meditation may provide comfort and encouragement, stimulate trust and perseverance, and facilitate sharing and dialogue. We "permit" the Word to speak as we listen and visualize, giving the Word time to speak in the silence.

Silence—or retained focus— is important to the dynamic of meditation. It goes with the slowed mental pace and internalized focus. Silence is also important to the meditative use of the Scripture. "Silence opens in us the space where the Word can be heard," says Nouwen. "Without reading the Word, silence becomes stale and without silence, the Word loses its recreative power. The Word leads to silence and silence to the Word."[18] Silence is the milieu of meditation in which we take in the Word. It is the environment of communion—of the "inner dialogue"—of listening, of seeing, and, consequently, of knowing.

3. Examples of Using the Word

In the vicissitudes and fluctuations of everyday life, we have a need as creatures bounded on all sides by our limits to hear a "word from the Lord." Devotional meditation provides such an opportunity—a milieu in which we can hear the voice of God and respond. Specific examples will best illustrate how the Scripture can provide the Word that we may need to hear.

When we become anxious because of uncertainties that weigh heavily upon us, we need to focus on Jesus' words, "Do not fear, only believe" (Mark 5:36). On the basis of this encouragement, this call from God, we may respond by surrendering our anxiety to the assurance of faith. It is one thing to own up to and accept our anxieties, but it is another to "hang on" to them. Once we have expressed our fears and accepted them, we can let them go.

If we encounter a spate of disappointments and a dearth of satisfactions, we may be tempted to become discouraged and experience spiritual fatigue. Then it is helpful to listen to Jesus' invitation, "Come to me, all who labor and are heavy laden, and I will give you rest" (Matt. 11:28). The fluctuations of our lives are reminders of our dependency. Man in his arrogance has chafed under this dependency and sought in innumerable ways to escape from it. But there is no escape.

Realistically, the alternative is to accept our creatureliness. We are not our own creator, so being aware of our dependency is normal; expressing this dependency is expressing our humanity; and coming to Jesus to receive his rest is acknowledging our source.

There are times when we may lack the courage to do what needs to be done. All kinds of pressures may be exerted on us to conform to the world. We may be threatened by the loss of job or promotion or loss of relationships and friends if we affirm where we stand on matters of honesty and justice. Then we need to be clear about our priorities. Meditating upon the parable of the pearl of great price may disperse our confusion (Matt. 13:45-46). A pearl, symbolizing the kingdom of God, is discovered buried in a field. In order to secure the pearl, the discoverer sold everything he had to buy the field. It was worth it.

At times we may attempt to solve the dilemma by indecision. Indecision, of course, is a misnomer; it simply means that we put off a decision until one is made for us. What we need in this temptation is a directive to action. Meditating upon a directive may release the power of decision. "Submit yourselves therefore to God. Resist the devil and he will flee from you" (James 4:7). Under God we have more power than we think, and listening to these words may clarify our potential.

Since we decide—in one way or another, indecision not withstanding—we need to decide consciously to take responsibility for our lives under God. Any postponement of a choice that could be made now is a compromise with our identity. We need to focus on the present as the moment for decision. "Behold, now is the acceptable time" (II Cor. 6:2). Meditating upon these words could stimulate the courage needed to take the risks of conscious decision.

Problems of decision are not always due to a lack of

courage. Sometimes we "lack a vision" which would give us a sense of direction in making decisions. "Where there is no vision, the people perish" (Prov. 29:18 KJV). A song from "South Pacific" puts it in the positive: "You have to have a dream to make a dream come true." Although there is no allotted dream or vision in the Word for each person, there is the assurance of a calling for each. God calls us to live our lives purposefully in this world. Once we have integrated ourselves around our calling, things "fall into place." Our decisions follow the rationale of our values and priorities which are reflected in our approach or attitude toward life.

The Old Testament story referred to in a previous chapter concerning the people of God who left their bondage to journey toward their promised homeland is a helpful focus for meditation when we need guidance in moments of decision-making. Arriving at their destination, but fearing an encounter with the inhabitants of the land, God's chosen people lost their nerve, and so they wandered in the wilderness for forty years. After the death of that generation, the next generation accepted the risks of entering the new land, leaving the old pattern of aimless wandering.

This story is pivotal in the Old Testament because it illustrates the power of decision to shape human destiny. It is—according to the Epistle to the Hebrews—the story of each person's pilgrimage through life. We all face the decision of whether we shall wander in the wilderness of fear and indecision—going in circles of futility—or whether we shall respond in faith to our calling to leave that which is old and enter into the new. With this background in mind, meditating upon the Epistle's exhortation may help us to "see" the context within which we make our decisions. "Today, when you hear his voice, do not harden your hearts as in the day of rebellion" (Heb. 3:15). "Let us therefore strive to enter that rest, that no one fall by the same sort of disobedience" (Heb. 4:11).

There may be periods in our life when a "low self-image," which seems to inflict so many in our culture, comes down heavily upon us so that we find it difficult to experience forgiveness and experience instead inadequacy and worthlessness. In commenting on Karl Menninger's book, "Whatever Happened to Sin?" a friend said, "A more important question is, whatever happened to forgiveness?" Although forgiveness is at the heart of the Christian gospel, it has proved to be a difficult teaching to appropriate. The believer may have it "straight" in his head, but in his heart he may continue to feel rejected. By moving our head into our heart, meditation may be a way to bring forgiveness into the center of our being.

When Jesus' enemies cruelly used a woman convicted of adultery to force him to say whether he followed the law of judgment or of mercy, he evaded their trap by saying, "Let him who is without sin among you be the first to throw a stone at her" (John 8:7). When her accusers left and Jesus was alone with her he said, "Neither do I condemn you; go, and do not sin again" (John 8:11). When we feel a sense of guilt and self-condemnation, we need to hear Jesus say these words to us also. A reenforcing word from Romans provides a good follow-up. "There is therefore now no condemnation for those who are in Christ Jesus" (Rom. 8:1). In meditating upon these Scriptures we permit their content to inform our hearts as well as our heads so that the assurance of God's forgiveness may move us also to forgive ourselves. Once we come to an acceptance of ourselves through forgiveness, we will become aware of an important by-product of this acceptance—we will be less critical, less judgmental, of others. Much of our lashing out at others is a projection onto them of our dissatisfaction with ourselves.

Not all selections of Scripture for meditation should be based on our needs of the moment. In fact, most of the time we

Let the Spirit In

will probably use the Scripture for "maintenance" rather than "repairs." An area where we need continual "maintenance" is in our personal relationships—particularly our family relationships. How do we keep love operative in these relationships? St. Paul's well-known description in I Cor. 13:4-8 of how love operates—or is inoperative—is a meditative base which can assist us in our caring one for another. His initial description of how love operates is positive. "Love is patient and kind." This is followed by specific descriptions of how love is violated. "Love is not jealous or boastful; it is not arrogant or rude. Love does not insist on its own way; it is not irritable or resentful."

In contrast to the initial description in which one's imagination is stimulated to envision patience and kindness, these latter descriptions are negations rather than affirmations. I find it helpful to "listen" to these negations and then imaginatively cancel each descriptive word or phrase by projecting a huge "X" through it as a symbol of its negation.

The concluding descriptions are climactic in nature. "Love does not rejoice at wrong, but rejoices in the right. Love bears all things, believes all things, hopes all things, endures all things. Love never ends." These descriptions give positive directions and positive assurance. In the fluctuations that characterize our intimate relationships we need such assurances to persist in our hopes and endeavors.

4. Knowledge of the Bible

In providing these examples of how we can use the Scripture in our meditation, it is obvious that I am presupposing some knowledge of the Scripture in a day when such knowledge is decreasing. My own religious instruction strongly emphasized memorization of specific passages and disciplined reading of the Bible. I realize that neither of these emphases are in vogue today. Consequently, you may be wishing for assistance in the use of the Bible. Such assistance is usually provided by churches through their education programs. We need the knowledge of biblical scholars to enlighten us on linguistic, textual, and socio-historical matters. While it is fine to have an authority to lead us, some of the most effective Bible study groups are those where each person, in addition to the leader, teaches and learns from the others. We need one another, as members of the body of Christ, for our understanding of the Scripture. It is through such sharing that we support, encourage, and "pastor" one another. So if you feel the need of help in securing knowledge of the Bible, I would suggest that you investigate the classes and groups that are available in your church or community. If none exists, contact your pastor and see if you can assist him or her in beginning such a class.

Though devotional meditation is focused on one's inner life, its context is life with the body of Christ. In the act of meditating we are one in spirit with the worshiping, witnessing, and caring community of believers. Obviously we can discern our relationship to the body when we meditate in a group setting, as some of you may be doing in the reading of this book. But you can also have this awareness with you when you meditate alone. Think of yourself as a member of a body whose head is Christ and whose members minister one to another. Even when you are alone you are not really alone.

5. Conditioning Experience

As we meditate on Scripture and the Word becomes part of us, we are undergoing a conditioning experience. Since conditioning is associated with all sorts of behavior modification, it is frequently viewed with suspicion. We are not interested in being "brainwashed" by religion any more than by "Big Brother." On the other hand, conditioning is an inescapable influence in human development. We are "programmed" by our past experiences to act in specific ways in new experiences. In your family relationships, for example, have you noticed that you say and do things in a particular way when receiving specific stimuli with which you have had a long history? If your wife or husband criticizes you for something that you are hypersensitive about, you will probably react in the same way you have many times previously. In fact, you may even sound like your parents did under similar circumstances.

We would like to think we are free under God to change our behavior—to break with our previous conditioning. The Good News is that we are! But it is not easy. The old dies hard. Conditionings are broken not by freedom in the abstract, but by deciding to choose new conditionings. God has freed us through Christ from old bondages so that we might become servants of Christ. Freedom comes through commitment and not through independence. Recognizing our creatureliness means recognizing our dependency. Freedom for the creature lies in his or her commitment to the Creator.

Since conditioning is the way by which we are influenced in our functioning, our freedom centers on choosing our conditioning. The media—particularly television—are accredited with being the great "influencers" of our day. Jesse Jackson encourages black children to exercise their freedom to "turn off the tube." Agnes Sanford says she never watches television because she wants to control her own mind. Self-direction is considered a gift of God by the writer of II Timothy. "God did not give us a spirit of timidity but a spirit of power and love and self-control" (1:7). (Because in our day we may confuse "self-control" with "holding it all in," a better translation may be self-direction.) Meditating upon Scripture is an exercise in self-direction because we are choosing a means of conditioning ourselves to function in the direction of our commitment.

Like the pilgrim who meditated upon the Jesus Prayer until he began to hear his own heart saying the prayer, so also as our meditative conditioning continues we may "hear" the Scripture speaking to us from within. As we focus regularly on the Word at appointed times, we may "hear" and "see" it at unappointed times.

I have a friend who was critically injured in an auto accident. She was semiconscious for several weeks during which time she heard careless hospital personnel refer to her as having only a short time to live. During the same time she heard other words speak to her from her inner being: "I sought the Lord, and he answered me, and delivered me from all my fears." These words are from Psalms 34:4 which she had memorized years before in a confirmation class. In her dim awareness she interpreted them as a message to her that she would live. After her recovery she looked back on those words as having given her the hope she needed in her battle for life.

Recently I experienced a similar word from within in far less critical circumstances. In a sharp conflict with my teen-age son, I found myself repeatedly and unsuccessfully trying to "resolve" the conflict by saying, "What I said is final—that's it—period!" He reacted to my adamant attitude with passive and sullen resistance. Afterward I attempted to fortify my rightness with all sorts of justifications. In the midst of these I heard words from within saying, "Love does not insist on its own way." I was startled by their spontaneous entrance. I meditate on these words daily, but now they were coming to me beyond my conscious decision, and they were right on target!

I was not ready, however, to tell my son of any change in my approach. My pride was in the way. Fortunately he also was

Let the Spirit In

doing some rethinking about his role in the conflict. Before I got around to approaching him, he approached me with a compromise suggestion—and was quite taken back by my receptiveness. I had been prepared by the Word from within.

In devotional meditation the reasoning mind is not set aside but rather is slowed in its pace by the process of relaxation and is focused upon Scripture as a feeder of its thoughts. As these Scriptures are internalized through the conditioning effects of meditation, we are in effect "letting the mind of Christ be in us." Our mind is the locus of our reason—our thoughts—the rational base for our functioning. As the thought content of the Word takes shape within us, the mind of the Living Word is being formed within us.

6. A Brief Practice in Scriptural Meditation

We are ready now for a meditational exercise on the Scripture. Choose two of the biblical stories, parables, exhortations, or descriptions to which we have referred, or choose two scriptural meditations of your own selection. Begin again by relaxing through deep breathing, making the transition to the Holy Breath. Move from breathing to the abdomen. Feel the warmth and compassion it symbolizes. Then focus on your selected Scriptures one at a time. See the Word—hear it—listen to the Spirit. Allow a minute or two for this reflection. Then take your second selection and do the same. If there is any response on your part to the Scriptures—such as gratitude for their assurance or a longing for their fulfillment—direct this to God as a prayer. Do not read the next paragraph until you have concluded the meditation.

You may have been surprised at some of the insights or memories that entered your consciousness as you reflected on the specific Scriptures. In their constant interaction with things outside of us, our minds rarely have the opportunity to demonstrate their capacities for "inner dialogue." If you are meditating as a group, take some time to share with one another your response to the exercise. The inner dialogue shared by some may indicate that they are of a practical or rational bent—they received "ideas." Others may be mystical by nature and visually active—they received "pictures." If you were meditating alone, recount to yourself your reflections and observations as well as the conclusions you draw from them.

Let the Spirit In

Chapter Six

GUIDED DEVOTIONAL MEDITATION

Although it may be clear by now what I mean by devotional meditation, it may be well to recapitulate in preparation for a guided devotional meditation. If we meditate with the perspective of faith in God, then meditation is not simply something we do. With this perspective, meditation is also a response to God's direction—to our being called. Therefore I use the term devotional meditation to indicate this distinction. In this perspective we are creatures under God, and when we are in harmony with our Creator, we are in a position of optimum human functioning. It is my intention in this chapter to guide you in a devotional meditation. I will give directives throughout the meditation which you can read and follow.

You may wish to make a tape of this devotional meditation and use it as a learning device in your beginning meditations. Persons whom I have led in meditation have on occasion asked permission to tape the session and have said later that the tape served as a helpful structure for their meditating until they had worked out one of their own. If you would like to follow this procedure simply read the directing words into a tape recorder and time the silences indicated between them.

1. Building on the Previous Foundations

This guided devotional meditation will build on the foundations that we have laid in previous chapters. In the shorter exercises I provided instructions beforehand to guide you in your meditation. In this longer meditation I will provide directives during the meditation. The devotional meditation in which I will guide you is one I use in my own personal life as well as in pastoral counseling and in growth workshops. It can be used wholly or in part at any present moment as preparation for specific efforts, ordeals, and occasions. It can also be used as a disciplined devotional exercise on a daily basis. The purpose of providing a model is to help you to get started in a meditative discipline or to enhance—if such is desired—what you are already doing. From this model you will obviously add the creative insights that come from your own experience as you develop a model most fitted to you.

I will use the exercises that we have used previously to reach the meditative state. I wish to emphasize, however, that the characteristics of this state differ with individuals. The Silva Mind Control approach describes the meditative state as one in which alpha waves rather than beta waves emanate from the brain. Yet my Silva instructor said that some people seem to remain at the beta level in their meditation; so far as he was concerned this presented no problem. I would not concern myself with the frequency of the brain waves, and I believe that individual differences in the experience of meditation are not necessarily differences in the quality of meditation.

After the by now familiar initiating exercises, I will give a thought or suggestion or biblical picture and allow time for focusing and reflecting upon it. If you permit yourself you will become deeply involved in the meditation and may experience the restorative potential of this ancient religious practice. If you wish to tape the meditation, begin recording

Let the Spirit In

the directives in the next paragraph and follow the time allowances for silence. It may help to read the meditation through first so that you are familiar with it as you begin to record. After the recording is completed replay your own voice to guide you in the devotional meditation. If you choose not to tape, follow the directives as written, and as you meditate, estimate the times for silence rather than clocking them so that your concentration is unbroken. This meditation will take approximately twenty minutes.

2. The Guided Meditation Period

Get yourself into a comfortable position—with both feet on the floor and sit straightly on preferably a hard chair. When relaxed you will feel like you are sitting on a cushion. Rest your arms on your thighs. (silence—10 seconds)

Relax your body as a way of becoming open in spirit. (silence—10 seconds)

Drop your muscles, beginning with those in your feet. Drop your toes. Imagine the floor holding them up, pushing up against your feet. (silence—10 seconds)

Relax the calves of your legs, imagining the taut muscle fibers becoming loose. (silence—10 seconds)

Relax your knees. (silence—10 seconds) Relax your thighs, drop the muscles, let them go. (silence—5 seconds) Relax your back muscles, imagining them letting go, unraveling. (silence—5 seconds)

Relax your shoulders. (silence—5 seconds) Relax the muscles of your upper arm. (silence—5 seconds) Your elbows. (silence—5 seconds) The muscles of your forearm. (silence—5 seconds) Your fingers. (silence—5 seconds) It is said that if you are relaxed in your extremities—your fingers and your toes—you are probably relaxed throughout your body. So drop your fingers—each one separately. (silence—10 seconds)

Now very carefully and slowly rotate your neck on your shoulders, first in one direction, then in the other, so that your head rests balanced on your neck. (silence—10 seconds)

Relax your neck muscles, in front and back. (silence—5 seconds) When we are tense we clench our teeth and our jaws are tight. Relax your lower jaw. Let your teeth separate. (silence—10 seconds) Relax the muscles of your face. (silence—5 seconds)

If you have any health problems—a chronic pain, a malfunctioning organ, focus now in that area. Visualize the joint, muscle, or organ, and see it relaxing. (silence—20 seconds)

Imagine yourself floating in salt water (or clouds), being held up by the water (or the clouds). (silence—20 seconds)

Recall from your memory a peaceful scene—in nature, in church, in the family, with friends—and see that scene now. (silence—20 seconds)

Imagine your mind as being surrounded by walls like the ancient city of Jerusalem with watchmen posted on these walls who are alert, preventing any distracting thoughts from invading the meditative level. "Upon your walls, O Jerusalem, I have set watchmen; all the day and all the night they shall never be silent" (Isa. 62:6). (silence—20 seconds)

Focus now on your breathing—breathe deeply from the abdomen. (silence—10 seconds) Take in oxygen—let out carbon dioxide. (silence—10 seconds) The marvel of the body taking in life-giving air and giving off its wastes! (silence—10 seconds)

Breath and spirit are the same word in the Bible. So imagine breathing in the Holy Breath—Holy Spirit—and breathing out

Let the Spirit In

the obstructive and divisive spirits. (silence—10 seconds)

In the peaceful repose between exhaling and inhaling, hear the words from Isaiah, "Thou dost keep him in perfect peace, whose mind is stayed on thee, because he trusts in thee" (Is. 26:3). (silence—20 seconds)

Focus now on your abdomen. Let your exhalation take you there. (silence—10 seconds)

"Bowels of compassion"—splagna—intestines—the biblical symbol for warmth and tenderness. (silence—10 seconds)

"Be kind to one another, tenderhearted [abdomen], forgiving one another, as God in Christ forgave you." (Eph. 4:32) (silence—30 seconds)

Feel the affection in your abdomen for your loved ones. See each of them. Feel your affection for Christ. (silence—20 seconds)

"I yearn for you all with the affection [the intestines] of Christ Jesus" (Phil. 1:8). (silence—30 seconds)

A biblical symbol for God is the rock. "Lead thou me to the rock that is higher than I" (Ps. 61:2). (silence—10 seconds)

Picture Jesus' parable of the house built on the rock. See the winds blow against it—see it stand because of its solid foundation. (silence—20 seconds)

Now see the winds as stresses, memory-tapes, reverses— see yourself on the rock—but the stresses do not blow you off—cannot pull you off. If the stress winds blow hard, lie flat on the rock—you won't be blown off. (silence—10 seconds)

The Lord has not given us the spirit of timidity and fear, but of love, power, and self-direction (II Tim. 1:7). (silence—20 seconds)

Focus now on someone you care about who is hurting, either ill or emotionally disturbed, bereaved or in marital distress. See him/her or the marital relationship as he/she/it is—hurting, needing. Feel with the person or persons—identify with their pain. (silence—20 seconds)

Intercede for him/her/the couple. Imagine him/her/them healed, at peace, happy together—filled with the Spirit—with peace and joy. (silence—20 seconds)

Inwardly say amen to what you have seen—by faith. (silence—10 seconds)

Picture now a difficult situation in which you are involved, or someone close to you is involved—in your family, neighborhood, place of work, congregation. (silence—20 seconds)

See yourself/him/her functioning in this situation as you would hope you/he/she could—led by the Spirit. (silence—20 seconds)

"The fruit of the Spirit is love, joy, peace, patience, kindness, goodness, faithfulness, gentleness, self-control" (Gal. 5:22). (silence—20 seconds)

See yourself offering up your anxiety, your depression, to Christ. Let them go. See him taking them. (silence—10 seconds) Now see yourself filled instead with trust and enthusiasm. (silence—10 seconds)

"Trust in the Lord with all your heart, and do not rely on your own insight. In all your ways acknowledge him, and he will make straight your paths" (Prov. 3:5-6). (silence—20 seconds)

In a moment I will close the meditation with a prayer of the church, after which you may come out of the meditative state in a way natural to you. (silence—20 seconds)

"Grant us, O Lord, for our growth, thoughts that pass into prayers, prayers that pass into love and love that passes into eternal life, through Jesus Christ our Lord. Amen." (If you are taping, turn off the tape here.)

Let the Spirit In

This meditation may be expanded at several points. The intercession might include any number of persons, marriages, families, churches, peoples about whom you are concerned. Each is focused upon individually. Prayers for your own illnesses and pains can be offered by a similar use of mental imagery directed to God. Picture the area of your body that is ailing, then picture it again restored to healthy functioning, and say amen to it. If you can familiarize yourself with the physiology and anatomy involved in the illness and healing process, incorporate this knowledge into your imagery. Bible verses, parables, and stories that are especially meaningful to you can be added to or replace those that I have given.

Chapter Seven

DEVELOPING A DISCIPLINE

1. *The Process of Forming a Habit*

If you plan to continue with meditation you will become involved in the process of forming a habit. The formation period may be difficult since you will lack the support of familiarity. In addition, you will encounter resistance from old priorities. If you have been with a group in this study in meditation, you will have its support as you cultivate your own personal discipline. If you are alone, you may find yourself with no support other than your own determination. If you view your determination as a response to your faith—as a devotion to your calling—your determination will have considerable reenforcement.

As you begin, the momentum of your way of life will probably be in the opposite direction from the new habit you are attempting to form. Consequently, the strength of your determination may be a deciding factor in counteracting the natural forces that perpetuate old ways. The press of time, fluctuating interest, interruptions, and emotional "swings" may all conspire to thwart you. There is a point in the process, however—"a continental divide"—at which the momentum will begin to shift to the opposite direction. The natural resistance to what is new will begin to diminish as the new itself begins to form its own habit pattern. You will have a new support in your life as the discipline of meditation becomes familiar. What was formerly an oppositional force has now shifted to your side.

As you persist in your determination to form a meditational habit, soon your day will not seem complete without it. In Glasser's terms you are then "hooked" or positively addicted. Meditation will be a source of pleasure and stability as well as a symbol of daily security. The next stage in devotional meditation is to break with the addiction. It may not always be possible to meditate in any disciplined way. I have days when I have to make a choice between meditation and other opportunities or obligations, and I may choose against meditation. Because of its attraction this may be a difficult choice. One needs then to remind oneself that one's faith can function without meditation.

From this perspective devotional meditation is not a positive addiction. But if there is a positive addiction, it is an addiction to the presence of God, and God's presence is not dependent upon meditation. In a devotional sense meditation is a means—an important means—but not an end. If it becomes an end in itself, it has become identified in our minds with the presence of God. Yet God is not dependent upon any particular means to enter into our awareness. Addicts, even positive addicts, are not free. Those who worship the living God are free.

2. Encountering Problems

People who meditate discover common problems. One of these is finding the best time for meditation. After the habit is formed one can vary the time, but in initiating a discipline, having the same time each day is most important. Committing oneself to a specific time for meditation symbolizes its priority in one's life. It is also a defense against older, competing priorities. The morning hours seem to be the best time for most people. Meditating in the morning has the advantage of avoiding the unexpected interruptions that may occur as one's day enters its heaviest involvement. Mornings are also the prime time for meditation for setting the tone for the day, providing a daily orientation to one's values and priorities that may influence us during the day.

Some people, however, are not morning people. For various reasons they do not feel aware or alive until later in the day. In fact they may experience the peak of their functioning at night. One must discover one's own time in terms of one's personal characteristics, background habits, and family life as well as occupational obligations. I have discovered, for example, that the best time for me to meditate is not when the family is depending upon me for other responsibilities. To assume a higher priority for meditation at such times may result in more resentment than respect from those about us.

Normally I like to meditate in the morning shortly after rising. When this is not feasible, I work it in any time I can that does not infringe on my responsibilities to others. Sometimes I do it piecemeal, dividing my meditational format into separate parts—five minutes here, ten minutes there.

You may encounter disturbing thoughts and images as you meditate. Contrary to what you may surmise, meditation does not create the disturbance: rather meditation brings it into your awareness. In fact you are probably dimly aware that you have these conflicting thoughts and feelings. This may be one of the reasons some of us avoid getting too close to ourselves—why we may permit ourselves, for example, to become preoccupied with work and other activities. If you encounter disturbing images while you meditate you are actually one step ahead of where you were before in coming to grips with and resolving your conflicts. You may need to see your pastor or another counselor if the disturbing thoughts or

Let the Spirit In

images seem too painful to cope with alone. Your pastor may then have a suggestion concerning whether you should continue or cease meditation while engaged in the counseling process.

A common problem, not only at the beginning but even after the habit pattern is formed, is mind-wandering. There are days when one's concentration may be almost perfect and others when one may have difficulty focusing for more than a few seconds. Many factors may be involved in the difference, but one that I have noticed is the degree to which I am excited about something positive or disturbed over something negative. When these emotions are aroused they seem to claim my attention, and it requires much more effort than usual to block out distractions.

At these times we need to be patient with ourselves—tolerant toward our deficiency rather than discouraged. We can always use our freedom to return to the meditative focus once we realize that we have wandered, even though we may have to do so again and again.

The purpose of picturing our minds with watchmen on its walls at the beginning of the previous devotional meditation was to prevent mind-wandering. As we envision the watchmen, we are alerting ourselves to this potential hazard at the onset and directing ourselves to screen out distractions. Archbishop Bloom, following a procedure of St. John Climacus, suggests that one inform oneself at the beginning of a meditation of the time allotted for it. Then, regardless of how much of this time has been sabotaged by mind-wandering, we end the meditation at the set time. I have found a variation of this procedure helpful during periods of distraction, namely, to allot a certain amount of time to each of the distinctive parts of my devotional meditation. When each time allotment is up, I move to the next part even though I may not have succeeded in curbing my distraction sufficiently to complete the previous part. Knowing that we have limited our time, we are more apt to use it well than if it were open-ended.

In the beginning period of learning the discipline, some have a problem with drowsiness. In fact, I have had people go to sleep while I was leading them in a group meditation. If you are seated, particularly on a hard bottomed chair without arms, rather than lying on the floor or a bed, you are not as likely to be overcome with drowsiness. But it still may happen. Perhaps this is one reason why the Buddhist meditates in the lotus position. For beginners, at least, this position is too uncomfortable to permit drowsiness.

Sleepiness, of course, may be an indication that one is relaxed. The meditative state is between the state of sleep and the state of heightened awakenedness in which we interact with our environment. That we should slip off into sleep once we slow the mental pace of the wakened state should not be surprising. Sleepiness, however, is primarily an initial problem in meditating and tends to diminish as meditation becomes a disciplined habit. I find that meditation actually prevents me from going to sleep. Consequently, I do not meditate when I go to bed if I want to go right to sleep.

If drowsiness persists beyond the beginning period, it may be a form of escape from the intimacy with oneself that meditation precipitates. A person may have a subliminal awareness of disturbing realities buried deep within. Going to sleep has a long and relatively healthy history as a way of escaping when one's attention is moving too close to something that one is not ready consciously to attend to. If you are bothered by persistent drowsiness, try meditating early in the morning or late in the evening while taking a walk. Then, since you cannot go to sleep, see if any other escape mechanisms take over—such as mind-wandering.

Let the Spirit In

3. Practicing the Presence

Devotional meditation, as we have seen, is more than meditation. In words made memorable by Brother Lawrence in the middle ages, devotional meditation is a way of "practicing the presence of God."[19] It is a means of becoming aware of what is always present—a focusing on what is often left unfocused. In devotional meditation we position ourselves to receive from the Spirit, utilizing the means of receiving—the means of grace and the resources of our faith. The focus is on our "inner dialogue."

Meditation can strengthen our total person. This was Glasser's observation of secular meditation and the reason he called it a positive addiction. My caution concerning this term is confined to "addiction" and does not extend to the word "positive." Meditation has a positive influence on our relationships and activities. It reenforces our identity as sons or daughters of God.

In describing his confessional meditation, Fritz Kunkel says that the crucial question in determining the effects of such meditation is "practicing the presence of whom?"[20] Kunkel's answer is: "Not in the presence of a minister or a psychologist, but in the presence of God, things change completely." Meditation is a conditioning exercise in becoming; it is an integrating discipline for establishing whose we are. The "sine qua non" is the presence of God.

4. Redeeming Time

After the habit is formed, meditation can be done in a variety of ways and circumstances—while walking, resting, or riding, for example. We can also take the opportunity to meditate when we find ourselves in situations that do not require our full attention, such as unanticipated delays. There is no need for these waiting times to be frustrating. Instead of becoming upset when suddenly confronted with "time on our hands"—being engrossed in "killing time"—we can use these times to meditate. Time is too precious to be "killed"; rather it should be filled—and enjoyed. Impatience is phased out when we use these unanticipated delays productively. When blocked in our plans to do this or that, we can always focus on what Thoreau called "the frontier of the mind." We can reroute ourselves mentally and use a potential frustration as an opportunity to meditate. Besides developing the frontiers of our mind, meditation is much better for our health and disposition than seething with impatience.

5. By-Products of Meditation

There are important by-products to practicing the presence of God in meditation. They are by-products because the presence of God is the primary focus. We have emphasized one of these, namely health and healing, in previous chapters. Another is the ability to direct ourselves. Meditation is in itself an exercise in self-direction, which in the New Testament is described as a gift. As we have noted previously this description of self-direction as a gift is itself a scriptural focus for meditation. "God did not give us a spirit of timidity, but a spirit of power and love and self-control" (II Tim. 1:7). Listening repeatedly to this declaration of freedom helps us to claim for ourselves the gift which is offered to all.

The conditioning effect of devotional meditation can provide a greater freedom for us in which to function. It is frustrating to react to various stimuli in ways that we do not consciously affirm. Yet we know from many painful experiences how seemingly "automatic" and "instinctive" these reactions are. Where then is our freedom to act? In spite of our impression, these reactions are not instinctual or automatic. Rather they

Let the Spirit In

have been learned through much repetition. These bondages to re-acting are really holdovers from old conditionings. Under God it is possible—at least now and then—to become free to choose our responses to stimuli.

Meditation conditions us for this freedom because it assists us in overcoming a basic fear—a fear of ourselves. We are afraid of our lack of self-direction or self-control. We fear our affinity for being "hooked" by rage, panic, or depression when confronted by circumstances we feel we cannot handle. When we become "hooked," which happens most often in our intimate relationships, we react with unwise words and/or actions that are destructive to our basic intentions and desires, and that may also have a destructive influence on others. While we fear our potential for emotional and volitional chaos which can be triggered by forces beyond our control, self-direction, together with the love and power that accompany it, are gifts from God which we can receive. When the spirit of fear and timidity overtakes us, we can choose to remind ourselves that this spirit is from sources other than God.

In meditation we are making a choice to spend time with ourselves to focus on thoughts and symbols of a deeply personal nature. Meditation in itself is a highly self-directed activity and therefore an exercise in self-direction. Using our imagination, we can deal directly with our bondages by first reliving typical patterns of re-acting, then mentally cancelling these patterns and picturing ourselves following a different course of action in the same situation—one that we have chosen.

As meditation becomes a discipline in our lives, we will begin to feel at home with ourselves, for the disciplined time we spend with ourselves diminishes the fear of ourselves. The inner dialogue of meditation extends its influence beyond meditation. We take it with us as we enter into strange surroundings and new situations. This "inner familiarity" that

Developing a Discipline ◁ 85

Nouwen calls "being present to ourselves" is an antidote to loneliness. While we obviously need interaction with our surroundings and with other persons, we are not totally dependent upon them if we possess the ease and comfort of familiarity within ourselves.

In many things that happen to us we may have difficulty perceiving any influence from God. If he is present he is surely hidden! How then can we discern his presence? Certainly not by "sight" (II Cor. 5:7). By all evidence he is absent. Yet it is in precisely such barren circumstances that some have peceived his presence. God reveals himself in the most unlikely circumstances. He is not dependent upon any particular means of revealing himself; yet, in the record of his Word he has directed us to avail ourselves of the means through which he has chosen to reveal himself. Devotional meditation is one way of using these means. It is a way of sharpening the sensitivities of our faith to perceive his presence when some of our other sensitivities only perceive his absence. Our awareness of his presence, even in his "hiddenness," may make the difference at these times between a response of trust or a response of desperation, of security or of panic, of waiting or of sabotaging, of "the word fitly spoken" or of the word better left unspoken.

The effects of any discipline tend to be cumulative. Usually the effects are gradual so that one becomes aware of them only after one has ceased to anticipate them. Yet change has taken place. The discipline of devotional meditation is no exception.

POSTSCRIPT

Meditation as we use the term today is not simply another name for daily devotions. Although it is directed toward the same ends, it is a different activity. In fact, we Westerners might consider it a cessation of activity. The radical difference between Eastern forms of meditation and Western spirituality may have something to do with our current interest in Eastern religions—opposites, besides repelling, may also attract. "Yin" is drawn to "Yang."

I first heard about meditation with its contemporary meaning from a psychiatrist friend whom I had invited to lecture to one of my classes. He said that meditation had recently become a part of his life, and that it had meant a great deal to him. But I was somewhat in the dark about what precisely he meant by meditation, since I had always associated meditation with religion, and he seemed not to have had any religious accompaniment to his discovery. Later, after experiencing a tragedy in my life, I recalled his words about meditation. I was no longer satisfied with my previous format of daily devotions. Perhaps due to the academic nature of my vocation, my prayer times had become nine-tenths Bible "study." I even used the Greek New Testament rather than an English translation. There was much good in it, but now I needed to go beyond the cerebral to stabilize my life. So I sought out my psychiatrist friend. In a few informal sessions, he instructed me in his understanding of meditation. I was a good pupil because my long involvement in daily devotions had inclined me to disciplined activity.

I soon realized that meditation for my psychiatrist friend was more secular than religious, and that he had learned it at the Esalen Institute at Big Sur, California, under such teachers as Claudio Naranjo—considered by some to be the guru's guru. On a sabbatical leave to San Diego a couple of years later, I myself studied in the Human Potential Movement under Naranjo and several other teachers.

1. J. B. Pratt's Class in Thought Control

During this time I was surprised to hear my teachers refer to "pioneer movements" which were part of my own educational background, such as the early group therapy of Dr. Joseph B. Pratt, head physician of the Boston Dispensary, a "charity" out-patient clinic. As a graduate student I had spent a clinical semester with Pratt in his program which he termed a class in "Thought Control." Although Pratt worked with groups, his format was more similar to what is now called guided meditation than to group therapy. Selecting those patients from his Dispensary whom he perceived to have pronounced psychosomatic overtones to their ailments, he met weekly with them as a group. Following an informal discussion in which the patients were individually recognized, Pratt directed the group in a relaxation exercise. He did not interpret this exercise as meditation because at that time meditation was a word reserved for an ostensibly religious activity.

Pratt was an Episcopalian and quoted regularly from the then Archbishop of Canterbury, William Temple. Although he conducted himself as a physician and not as a priest, he did not hesitate to use religious resources in his relaxation exercises. First he taught us how to relax our bodies, beginning with our toes and continuing up our frames to our heads. We were seated on hard-bottomed, straight-backed

Let the Spirit In

chairs so that we would know we were relaxed when the hard seats felt like cushions. When we had completed the relaxation of our bodies, he "entered" our minds by directing us to imagine a peaceful scene. He provided suggestions— the shore of a lake, the top of a hill, a creek running through a woods. As we fixed our minds on a scene, he began slowly to recite the twenty-third Psalm, alternating each sentence with a moment of silence.

After the exercise was over, Pratt would occasionally discover to his delight that he had put a patient to sleep—a testimony of the patient's state of relaxation. Testimonies of healing were also not uncommon. One that I can still remember came from a faithful attender whom Pratt proudly described as a woman who had entered the class on crutches and now could walk without even a limp.

I was impressed with this exercise at the time and used it subsequently for my own needs and in my pastoral counseling ministry where it was especially useful to counselees with a high level of anxiety. For instance, there was a woman whose marriage was in a constant state of turmoil. Although her husband's repeated assurances of fidelity proved just as repeatedly to be false, she did not wish to leave him. How then could she endure this continuous strain? I directed her in the Pratt method of relaxation, and it seemed to help. Because of the context in which I had learned it, however, it was not until the contemporary interest in meditation that I was able to recognize his method as a form of meditation.

2. *Fritz Kunkel's Confessional Meditation*

Fritz Kunkel was another pioneer whose work played a significant role in my development. He was a psychiatrist who conducted a counseling program in a California church. Early in my teaching career I was introduced to his writings and for over a decade used his book "In Search of Maturity," as a text in my psychology of religion course.

Kunkel's stated purpose in this book was to place the insights of depth psychology, particularly those of Carl Gustav Jung, into a self-help format. He chose the term confessional meditation for his approach because of the specifically religious significance of these words. The context for confessional was the Confessional in Catholic churches in which parishioners confess their sins to a priest. The context for meditation was the traditional religious, mystical understanding of communion with God. In line with his self-help emphases Kunkel combined the terms by "removing" the Confessional from its orientation to a priest and associating it directly with the meditational orientation to the presence of God.

To assist the reader to confessionally meditate, he utilized Jung's concepts of the ego, the ego image, and the shadow. The ego, according to Kunkel's interpretation of Jung, is our distorted or off-center self which we associate with the word egotistic. The ego-image is the mental picture the ego forms of itself in order to maintain its security. The shadow is the ego's twin—but an opposing twin. Being a distortion of the self, and not the real self, the ego casts a threatening shadow. The shadow is a reminder of the ego's distortion. To use a metaphor, the sun as a symbol of God is directly in line with the real self. The ego, however, is to the side of the sun—or God—and hence creates a shadow self in the opposite direction. Whatever image the ego needs for its security— being unselfish or strong or right or independent or successful—is exposed by the shadow as an illusion. Therefore, for its own survival the ego needs to keep the shadow out of conscious awareness.

Kunkel diagrammed some of the typical ego/shadow conflicts to assist the reader in identifying his own ego state.

Having identified the conflict, the reader was encouraged to express all of his or her feelings associated with the conflict to God. With this protection, the ego and the shadow could confront and subsequently cancel each other out so that the real self buried beneath the conflict might emerge. For Kunkel this was not simply an introspective exercise, but rather a dialogical experience with God in whose presence "things change completely." It would be more accurate to say, "in our awareness of the presence of God, things change completely," that is, in the dynamic of confessional meditation.

Through the years each of these influences in my personal and professional development—daily devotions, Pratt's relaxation exercise, Kunkel's confessional meditation, the psychiatrist's instructions in meditation, and my own study in the Human Potential movement—have contributed to the evolving of my own approach to meditation.

NOTES

1. Herbert Benson, "Your Innate Asset for Combating Stress," *Harvard Business Review* (July/August 1974), 54.
2. Adam Smith, "Meditation Game," *Atlantic Monthly* (October 1975), 33–45.
3. William Glasser, *Positive Addiction* (New York: Harper, 1976), p. 79.
4. Cf. Stanton Peele's review of "Positive Addiction," *Psychology Today* (April 1976), 36, in which he states: "He [Glasser] offers no evidence or supporting reference for this model of how the brain operates. Nor does research indicate the brain works that way."
5. Quoted in Robert E. Ornstein, *The Psychology of Consciousness* (San Francisco, Cal.: W. H. Freeman, 1972), p. 121.
6. "Deep Breathing: More than a Sigh of Relief," *Prevention* (June 1978), 58–62.
7. Anthony Bloom, *Living Prayer* (Springfield, Ill.: Templegate Publishers, 1966), pp. 51–58.
8. *Ibid.,* p. 68.
9. Huston Smith, "Jesus Prayer," *Christian Century* (March 23, 1973), 363–66.
10. Henry Nouwen, *Reaching Out* (Garden City, N.Y.: Doubleday, 1975), p. 101.
11. Ornstein, pp. 120–21.
12. Nouwen, p. 105.
13. Ornstein, p. 103.
14. *Ibid.*
15. Nouwen, p. 106.
16. G. W. H. Lampe, *God as Spirit* (Oxford: Clarendon Press, 1977), p. 88.
17. Bloom, p. 59.

18. Nouwen, p. 97.
19. Brother Lawrence, *The Practice of the Presence of God* (Grand Rapids: Baker Book House, 1975).
20. Fritz Kunkel, *In Search of Maturity* (New York: Scribner's, 1951), pp. 259, 254.